LEABHAᴿᴵ ANN

ROSC

book sᵇ
ᵉᵉ'

'ate
by

MARK BRANDON READ

CHOPPER 4

MARK BRANDON READ

CHOPPER 4

HAPPINESS IS A WARM GUN

JOHN BLAKE

Published by John Blake Publishing Ltd, 3 Bramber Court,
2 Bramber Road, London W14 9PB, England

First published in the UK in hardback in 2004

ISBN 1 904034 38 1

British Library Cataloguing-in-Publication Data: A catalogue record for this book is
available from the British Library.

Design by www.envydesign.co.uk

Printed in Great Britain by Creative Print and Design (Wales),
Ebbw Vale, Gwent

1 3 5 7 9 10 8 6 4 2

Papers used by John Blake Publishing Ltd are natural, recyclable products made from
wood grown in sustainable forests. The manufacturing processes conform to the
environmental regulations of the country of origin.

Every attempt has been made to contact the relevant copyright-holders, but some were
untraceable. We would be grateful if the relevant people could contact us.

THE EDITORS

IN 1991 investigative journalist John Silvester interviewed Mark Brandon Read in Pentridge Prison's top security H Division for a series of newspaper reports. Over almost three years Read has written more than 1,000 letters from both inside and outside jail. These form the basis of Read's best-selling autobiography Chopper, its UK sequel How to Shoot Friends and Influence People and this book.

Silvester has been a crime reporter since 1978. He rowed at Cambridge (in a hired dinghy) and went to Oxford – on a bus.

Andrew Rule is a retired police reporter and failed amateur jockey who currently produces radio 3AW's award-winning breakfast programme.

The editors would like to thank Det. Sen. Sergeant R. O. T. Plumber (retired).

CONTENTS

THE STORY SO FAR

MARK Brandon 'Chopper' Read is a self-confessed killer and standover man who may spend the rest of his life in Tasmania's Risdon Prison for a crime he declares he did not commit. He was sentenced to an indefinite term 'at the Governor's Pleasure' in 1993 over a shooting near Launceston the previous year.

Read has spent most of his adult life in prisons – including more than ten years in Pentridge's notorious H Division. After his release from Pentridge in 1990 he became a best-selling author, publishing three volumes about his life and crimes.

Read's success sparked outrage, and even threats to legislate to stop criminals from profiting from writing autobiographies. He sought permission from prison authorities to write a fourth book, but it was officially denied. He was further angered when denied permission to marry his fiance, Mary-Ann Hodge. He threatened to take the issue to the United Nations but then decided to revert to type and smuggle out material for the book under the authorities' noses. Chopper Read now faces punishment, including possible solitary confinement, for refusing to buckle to the order to stop writing.

Read says himself: 'The last bloke who got his jollies burning books was a little Nazi called Adolf, and it didn't get him too far.'

The criminal predator who abducted and tortured drug dealers for a living, maintained he'd retired from crime when he went to Tasmania in 1990. He could have lived a comfortable life with the royalties from his books, but virtually all the money has been spent on a lengthy legal campaign to have him released. But while he has lost his liberty and his money, the irrepressible Read has maintained what he calls his 'scallywag sense of humor' and his telling observations of an underworld sub-culture that most people never see.

PREFACE

THE Governor called me into his office one fine day and in his best serious voice with his best serious look told me I could no longer write letters to my publishers because it appeared to him I was trying to write another book. The man should have been a rocket scientist.

He handed me back a small pile of mail that I had written and posted off to my publishers over the previous ten days. He was quite friendly and nice about it, but quite firm: I did not have permission to write books.

This was in spite of the fact that I had already written two books while being held in the prison's remand yard, and neither attacked the jail or breached the security or good management of the prison.

I find it slightly comic that after nearly two years of suspecting that I was smuggling my literary efforts out of the prison it suddenly dawned on the prison hierarchy that my books had been written through the prison mail: one letter at a time, one page at a time, all carefully read, censored, and cleared by prison security.

The Governor told me that if I wished to write a book I must apply in writing to the general manager of the prison and permission might be granted. However, prison security made it quite clear that even if permission was granted that virtually all mail sent out by me aimed toward any future book or literary effort would be deemed to be in 'bad taste' or 'inappropriate', or morally or politically incorrect. Meaning that any remarks about the prison or its management or matters relating to the police, the courts or the administration of justice in general would be blocked.

That means I would be able to write about recipes, the weather and not much else. So, taking all that into consideration, and bearing in mind that I am no longer in the remand yard and allowed the phone calls and other small freedoms permitted to men held on remand, I was left wondering if it was worthwhile trying to write a fourth book.

I tried to do the right thing, and wrote to the prison general manager and the Governor, but I knew the deck was stacked against me from the start. Even if I got so-called 'permission' my letters would be gutted.

Some of my outgoing mail had already been stopped because I had made comic jests and light-hearted remarks that some genius decided came under the heading of 'sexual innuendo'. Checking the mail for cash and drugs I can understand, but reading every word and making moral judgements on the content is Monty Python madness.

I've had dozens upon dozens of letters stopped. Even poetry was not allowed, until wiser heads prevailed at the top. One prisoner even had his incoming mail stopped because it was perfumed, for God's sake.

Imagine how I felt. After knocking out three national bestsellers under very difficult conditions it would have been just as easy to give the game away. I am amazed that in a so-called democratic country that any citizen, whether a prisoner or not, can effectively be forbidden from writing.

I tried to explain that the whole thing was just too much bloody bother and I was no longer interested. I've done three books, and got Governor's Pleasure for it. If I get another one out, I said, I'll probably get the chair ... and I don't mean a Chair of Literature at a university.

This mindless hysteria over a fourth book is laughable. It's not as if anything I've got to say relates in any way to the running of the prison. It is a case of prison security and the jail administration going beyond what they are required to do. They have become literary police.

If the authorities tried to stop some government-subsidised, black tee-shirt wearing academic trendy, of questionable sexuality, from writing some boring 60-page book about the mating habits of Tibetan yaks, the civil libertarians would be protesting in the streets.

But because the author is a Good Ol' Boy with no ears, who is popular with the book-buying public, and therefore not seen as trendy, then no-one has lifted a finger.

It appears that the principle of freedom of speech upheld in the constitution and law of every truly democratic country, falls short south of Bass Strait. At least, in the case of Mark Brandon Read it does.

I see this as a blatant attempt to gag me. I suspect it is a breach of the United Nations Charter on the humane containment of prisoners, and I know Amnesty International has strong views on freedom of speech and censorship. Didn't the Russians use to pull similar stunts with their wayward writers? I may not be Alexander Solzhenitsyn, but even if I am only a tongue-in-cheek sarcastic ratbag, bar-room story teller and dunny wall poet, so were Banjo Paterson and Henry Lawson.

I want to continue being a tongue-in-cheek, sarcastic, ratbag story teller and dunny wall poet, and I shouldn't have to ask permission to continue and I should not be the victim of censorship. I would be the only Australian author ever to have these third world, Iron Curtain restrictions imposed on him.

In Australia it is considered perfectly wonderful to talk at length about what you would like to do, and providing you never do it no man will raise his voice against you. But if you get off your arse and get out there and actually do it the critics will knock you.

Criminals are told to pick themselves up, dust themselves off, and improve themselves. But the very, very few who have tried to do just that are widely condemned.

No-one ever dreamed of declaring the money earned from writing a book to be classed as the 'profits of crime' until I came along. But when the politicians saw that a crook could not only write books but national bestsellers that appealed to the common man, a law was created to try to stop me.

Do the brain-dead politicians think that I would grab a drug dealer, and then shorten his shoe size because I thought that one day it may make a slightly amusing anecdote in a book? I have just tried to tell my life story, warts and all, and if I make an honest dollar along the way, so what? Now they are even trying to stop that.

Criminals are told to mend their ways and improve themselves, but when we do, the rules get changed. The people who run the game not only have the umpires in their pocket, but they move the bloody goal posts half way through the match. How can you win?

Sometimes while writing this I have been at the end of my tether and tempted to quit . . . but then I'd think about the small army of friends and loved ones who are with me in their hearts and minds. And that's when I decided it would be more fun to sneak the letters out, just to shove it up the authorities.

You're holding the result in your hand. Please pay at the counter.

Mark Brandon Read

CHAPTER 1

THE SEMI-MENTAL BLOKE

(APOLOGIES TO C. J. DENNIS)

PISS Ant was a tough little thief from Carlton. He was barely five foot tall, and so the nickname Piss Ant was slightly unkind, but it fitted.

However, Piss Ant made up for his lack of height with great physical strength. In tests of youthful guts and strength he shocked all us kids with his ability to stick a large needle into a very private part, indeed.

We stared in horror the first time Piss Ant did this trick. I went first, stabbing the needle through my cheek, in one side and out the other. Dave the Jew pushed the same large needle through his left hand and thought he had won the game. Then Piss Ant pulled his dick out and said 'give me the needle'.

Needless to say Piss Ant won the pain game, with no-one wishing to take up the challenge. How could you compete with a bloke as mental as that? He once carried me on his shoulders on a three mile walk from the Bush Inn Hotel on the corner of Williams Road and Malvern Road, Prahran, to Richmond Railway Station, with the Jew egging him on all the way.

I weighed fourteen and a half stone back then and Piss Ant weighed nine, but all of it was rock hard muscle. He would do 100 one-armed push ups in a row, either arm. He prided himself on his strength. He had a classic little man's complex, not to mention a killer right hand uppercut that, providing he got in first, would knock out most blokes with one punch.

Piss Ant had several sisters, all younger than him and all taller, which was a never-ending embarrassment. So, to make up for it, he would regularly give each sister a sound flogging for the slightest reason. Piss Ant's sisters almost stood to attention when he walked in the door.

While not agreeing with Piss Ant's treatment of his sisters, I must say they were the dumbest girls I have ever encountered, and all of them were famous dirty girls.

Piss Ant was not in our mob, the Surrey Road gang, but he was a mate of Cowboy Johnny Harris, having at one stage attended the same school. What school and where, and for how long, I was never told. But somehow Piss Ant and the Cowboy knew each other well and liked one another. Piss Ant's mother was in prison doing a ten-year stretch and his dad was dead. More than that we were never told. Their old grandfather was a Scotsman who fought in the First World War in France, and a staunch member of the Orange Lodge's Black Chapter. He was a lovely old chap but a little bit dippy. I will never forget that he was born in 1898, as he was two years older than the year, meaning that in 1972 he was 74 years old. Old Robbie was a good old guy and, to be honest, the only one in the whole family I considered even half sane. He is dead now, poor old fella. This is but an introduction to the main event and a story that took place in 1977, involving myself, Vincent Villeroy, Dave the Jew and the mad family of the Piss Ant and old Rob.

The whole thing took only a weekend but it taught me a valuable lesson, and that is that because the whole world seems insane to get ahead you simply have to be madder than the next guy.

It all started like this . . .

Old Rob was fond of a drink and would ring Piss Ant to come and get him when he got himself too drunk to walk. One Friday night myself, Vincent Villeroy and Dave the Jew were having a drink in the Tower Hotel in Collingwood, with Dave drinking tomato juice. The bar room door opened and in walked Piss Ant, and asked if we had seen his grandad, which we had not. We all went outside to help Piss Ant find him, as we all knew and liked old Rob. We were quite amused and puzzled to find a wheelbarrow on the footpath with a blanket and a pillow in it – and further shocked to see Piss Ant grab the handles and push it off.

It turns out that Piss Ant had taken to fetching grandad with the wheelbarrow. The old bloke would lie in the barrow with the pillow under his back and the blanket under him so as not to get his clothes dirty, and a drunk and sleepy Piss Ant would wheel him home, a sound idea if not just a wee bit comic.

When grandad said he was on the wagon, he actually meant in the wheelbarrow pushed by his grandson. However, old Rob was a wanderer and had taken to walking from Fitzroy to Collingwood, getting blind drunk and ringing Piss Ant to come and pick him up. Grandad would not travel by taxi as he believed it was highway robbery, and Piss Ant did not own a car, hence the wheelbarrow. We all walked up to the Gasometer Hotel and there was old Rob pissed and fast asleep on the footpath, having been tossed out. He was quite a sight.

Vincent Villeroy wanted to call a taxi but Piss Ant said; 'what about the wheelbarrow'.

'Forget the dam barra,' pleaded Vinnie, but old Rob had woken up and was sitting up in the barrow like a jack-in-the-box and having plenty to say. He would not hear of a taxi and pointed one arm forward like Hannibal on his elephant, and yelled: 'Home laddie!'. And Piss Ant pushed away.

What the hell, we thought, and all walked along with Piss Ant and the old man in the wheelbarrow, drinking cans of beer all the way from the Gasometer Hotel in Collingwood to Fitzroy.

It is a good long walk, let me tell you, and Piss Ant only rested twice if you don't count the red lights. It was an hour's walk, or so it seemed. Piss Ant may have been a tough, bad-tempered little ratbag but he loved his old grandfather.

It was about 11pm when we got to the home straight. Piss Ant's youngest sister opened the door. The other sisters were working at a massage parlor in St Kilda, although they had told grandad they worked as mail sorters at Australia Post. Old Rob believed whatever he was told. Piss Ant and Vincent put him to bed and later we all sat in the kitchen, drinking. The chit chat turned to the wedding of Piss Ant's best friend, Head Butt Larry. I won't mention his last name. The wedding was Sunday afternoon and the buck's night was Saturday night.

What with a little bit of talking and quite a lot of drinking we stayed up all night. We were all still in the kitchen drinking whisky, with Dave the Jew eating steak and eggs that Piss Ant's little sister had cooked for him.

All-night drinking sessions were a way of life for us and a quiet drink in the quiet wee hours was a delight we all enjoyed. Piss Ant's other sisters came home just before dawn. They were knackered after a hard night in 'the office'. They were bleach blonde, heavily-made up, bad mouthed dumb molls who swore like drunken sailors. Naturally, being gentlemen, we were very pleased to see them.

After the hellos and kisses of greeting all round and the sisters' delight in seeing my sawn-off shotgun sitting on the kitchen table and Dave the Jew's .38 revolver next to it, the conversation again turned to Head Butt Larry's wedding and the Saturday night bucks' party.

Etiquette demanded, of course, that as best man Piss Ant had to provide the stripper to put on a show and turn it on for the boys. He was having a problem finding a girl, as he was too cheap to pay the going cash rate, and neither of his two prostitute sisters were able to con any of their girlfriends into it.

The youngest sister did not work in a parlor as she stayed home to keep house and look after grandad. Piss Ant looked at her, the biggest and by far the best-looking of the sisters and, as cool as a cucumber, said: 'Well, I guess you are it.'

'How come whenever you need to butter someone up I end up becoming the butter?' replied the kid sister.

I thought Piss Ant would smack her in the mouth but he only laughed. Me and Dave and Vinnie were not invited to the wedding but Piss Ant invited us to the bucks' turn. We were close, but obviously not that close. When he asked us to come along his sister said, 'Well that's okay. At least I will have three good guys on my side. Head Butt and his crew are a bunch of madmen.'

This should have been a warning to me because Piss Ant's whole family were mad, and if this Head Butt Larry was madder than them it was saying something. The bucks' night was to be held at a house in Richmond. This also should have been another warning as we did not get on good with the Richmond boys, and Head Butt Larry was a Richmond boy, as well as a madman. Not a good combination. The danger signs were there well before the night began, but I was too stupid or too pigheaded to take notice of them.

After sunrise we called a taxi and all went back to South Yarra. Dave and Vinnie dropped me off at Rockley Road and Vinnie went off with Dave to have a sleep at Dave's place.

I went to bed after my old Dad cooked me breakfast of sausages and eggs smothered in black pepper washed down with a big mug of Milo. I slept like a log until about six o'clock that evening, when Dad woke me up to say Dave had arrived and was sitting in the lounge room.

I showered, shaved and dressed and with Dad's help armed myself for the night, then Dave and I took a taxi back to Dave's place to collect Vincent, who was playing chess with Dave's Dad.

We had to wait a further half hour for the chess game, which had a $100 bet riding on it. Dave's Dad won. Vinnie never could beat Dave's Dad at chess; none of us could. We all headed off to Vinnie's place in Port Melbourne and collected his old Pontiac car, a big old Yank Tank.

Vincent didn't like going out half dressed on a Saturday night, so he went inside and collected his old 9mm Luger semi-automatic handgun. It was then that I started to feel ill-at-ease about what the night held in store. But it was too late to have second thoughts. We headed off to the address at Laity Street, Richmond.

As we got near the house, Dave said to Vinnie, 'keep driving.' I asked what was wrong. Dave had recognised a white GT Falcon belonging to the brother of a well-known Richmond hood who had been in a gang fight in Richmond in 1974, resulting in my near death and the death of our old and dear friend Cowboy Johnny Harris.

The Jew had put the gentleman concerned and two others on the missing list over the matter. We parked around the corner and added the situation up. Piss Ant was the Cowboy's friend and too dumb to put a set up like this together. We guessed that news of our invitation to the bucks' night had reached the ears of certain Richmond gentlemen, and they had either gatecrashed or had been invited because they were friends of Head Butt Larry's.

Nevertheless, Piss Ant had invited us to a dangerous situation, but we decided to attend anyway. We drove to the Royal Oak Hotel and I rang 'Loxy', my old mate Robert Lochrie, and told him to meet us at the Laity Street address. He was drinking at the Dorset Gardens Hotel with another mate, Frankie, at that stage the most feared stand up street fighter in the eastern suburbs. Loxy agreed to be at the party in an hour's time with Frankie, and two car loads of what was drunkenly referred to as Loxy's crew. We drank at the Royal Oak for a half an hour with old Tommy Ballis, then left to attend the party, waving a friendly goodbye to old Tommy, who worked at the pub.

We drove slowly to Laity Street, parked at the end of the street and walked towards the house. We were greeted by a handful of the Richmond boys, who gave us a very false friendly welcome. I felt like General Custer must have just before he got an Indian haircut.

Alarm bells rang in our heads. The set up was on. We went inside and there were about 50 to 60 men in the house with about 30 of them in the lounge room drinking and about the same number in the kitchen, also drinking. About ten minutes later Piss Ant came in and greeted us. He was totally unaware of any ill-will or bad feeling or any set up. Henry Kissinger, he was not.

Head Butt Larry was in the lounge room with the Richmond gentleman who owned the white GT, a well-known knockabout would-be Richmond gangster, who, for the sake of this story, I will call Leo the Lion.

Leo spotted Dave the Jew. He could hardly miss him ... he was the only one in the house wearing a Yarmulka, or Jewish skull cap. The tension between the two men was chilling, but the party was in full swing, with Piss Ant's sister dancing about in high heels and schoolgirl's uniform with a dress that hung a few inches below her bottom.

It was a full striptease routine with Larry sitting on a chair in the middle of the lounge. Dave and Vincent had their eyes on Leo and I was trying to keep my eye on both the girl and Leo.

Leo could not keep his eyes off the girl. She had the buttons of the school uniform open and was rubbing a substantial set of tits into Head Butt Larry's face. It was then I noticed that Larry had his hands cuffed behind the back of the chair, just to make it interesting.

To make it more interesting, she was undoing Larry's pants, and his excited condition was evident, much to the cheers and laughter of the onlookers. Several men watching the performance exposed themselves and the stripper was encouraged to greater heights.

As she proceeded to sit on Head Butt's lap and ride him like a jockey, Piss Ant told the crowd to stand clear and let her ride Larry to the finish. Larry's handcuffs were undone and the cheers were loud and long. Little sister seemed to love the attention.

She then walked through the crowd and into the bedroom. As she walked past Dave the Jew she kissed him on the cheek and whispered in his ear. Then she went into the bedroom and yelled 'One at a time, you blokes!'

As the party goers queued to take their turn, I joined Dave and he whispered, 'She told me to watch my back.' The Richmond boys were gathering around Leo the Lion, but seemed to be in two minds about what to do first, attack us or pump the girl.

By this time she had attended to at least six of the Richmond boys and was yelling out 'hurry up'. No doubt she was just telling their fortunes. She must have had a stop watch in there with her. I was standing with Dave and Vincent when Piss Ant came over and said 'What's going on?'

No sooner had the words got out his mouth than Loxy and Frankie, with about a dozen drunken ratbags armed with cricket bats, lengths of iron pipe and broken bottles, came crashing through the front door, smashing everything in sight.

To quote Sherlock Holmes, the game was afoot. Dave attacked Leo and started pistol whipping him to the ground. I fired one blast from my sawn-off shotgun into the ceiling of the loungeroom, then started smashing the barrel of the gun into the faces of anyone in my road.

Old Vincent, a former heavyweight boxer, was sending men crashing to the floor with lefts and rights. Someone hit the Jew over the head with a bottle. Vincent decked the offender with a right hand that would have killed a horse.

By this time Loxy had made his way to the loungeroom. Frankie and the Croydon Boys, from the Dorset Gardens pub, were making short and bloody work of the rest of the party goers.

Head Butt Larry had his collar bone broken. Leo the Lion lost an eye and nearly all his teeth. Poor Piss Ant just sat in the lounge totally nonplussed. The party had turned into the bucks' night from hell. 'Was it the dips?' he must have wondered.

At the finish of things we all headed for the front door with Piss Ant's sister yelling 'I'm coming with you guys.' Poor Piss Ant was helping his friend Head Butt to his car. The whole thing was chaos. Me, Dave and Vinnie with the girl in her school uniform, all jumped into Vinnie's old Pontiac and, followed by Loxy and Frankie and their crew, drove to the Rising Sun Hotel to gather our thoughts.

We regrouped in the bar and checked our injuries. Razza had a broken nose, Fatty Neil a broken arm, Loxy had busted two knuckles and, more importantly, lost his cricket bat, and Dave the Jew had blood coming out his head. Vincent had broken his new watch and I had somehow lost my left shoe. A good Hush Puppy is hard to find. There were assorted cuts and black eyes with a few fat lips tossed in, but all in all sixteen men against nearly 60 had won the night.

We were all standing around the stripper, who was barefoot and wearing nothing but a short school uniform. If we were going to get arrested that night it would be if the police saw us with her, as she looked like a cheerful rape victim.

As we left the Rising Sun and got into our cars, two shots rang out and hit Loxy's car. No-one was hit, but it made us very angry. A car chase started up, and took us at speeds of 70 to 100 miles per hour from Richmond across the river down Chapel Street, Prahran, where the car we were chasing sideswiped another car turning a corner.

The driver and passenger got out and ran. We headed them off and got them outside the College Lawn Hotel, where Dave the Jew pistol-whipped both. We held them until they lay in a bleeding unconscious mess on the concrete.

The night was over. All good things must come to an end. As my Mum used to say, you should always leave a party before the end so that you can remember the good times. Mind you, I don't think she meant the sort of good times we'd had that night. Loxy and Frankie took Piss Ant's sister home, probably to lick her wounds. Dave, Vincent and myself went back to Vinnie's place and sat and pondered the night's events. In a strange way it was Johnny Harris coming back to say hello, as the whole thing had really started in 1974 when the Cowboy was killed. For me, it was just one more reminder that the ghosts of the past will always be there ready and waiting to pounce on me when I least expect it.

It was the last blue we ever had that could be attributed to the death of Cowboy Johnny and the revenge that followed. As stories go it's not one of the best or the bloodiest, but for me it's a blue I've always remembered.

Vincent Villeroy died in 1990 in his home town of Londonderry, Northern Ireland. Piss Ant died in a traffic accident in South Australia in 1984. His grandad returned to Scotland in 1988 to attend his brother's funeral and died there a fortnight later, aged 90 years.

Piss Ant's baby sister got married and, I understand, lives a good life. But two of the other sisters weren't so lucky. They both died of heroin overdoses in St Kilda massage parlors within a year of each other.

Frankie had three heart attacks in a row and is no longer the raging bull he once was. Loxy is still alive and well, even though he was recently stabbed. Dave the Jew is still going strong. And Cowboy Johnny Harris, as readers know, had his ashes poured into the Prahran Swimming Pool late one night in 1974, after which Dave and I gave him a 21-shot salute with a sawn-off .22 rifle.

As I sit in cell 42 in C Yard of Risdon Prison, all I seem to have is my memories. Nothing that happens these days seems the same as it once was, and while I live in the present I constantly miss the dead friends of old. All my life people have been coming into my life leaving their mark on my mind, heart and soul, and then dying on me or vanishing into the mists of time. It makes me sad and sentimental.

Loxy contacted me recently and told me that he would step

forward and say that he shot Sid and go to jail, and I would walk free. It was a stupid idea, but this is the blood loyalty of the men I call brothers and friends. When I lose them it haunts me forever.

If my four books could be dedicated to anything or anybody, I dedicate them to my dead friends.

CHAPTER 2

HOW TO BLUE WITHOUT BLOODSHED

SO it's come to this, as Ned Kelly said shortly before they stretched his neck. Chopper Read, the streetfighting lunatic who waged the legendary Pentridge 'Sausage War'* that left a trail of Australia's hardest crims maimed and mutilated, has taken on debating.

Now, those who know me well will tell you I love a bit of a debate, although they might also say I like to finish the discussion with a baseball bat or a blow torch. I have found in the past that lethal weapons tend to get opponents to see the logic of your argument.

But in a debate like this, under the Gentlemen's Rules here at Risdon Prison, pride of the Tasmanian penal system, the only weapon allowed is the gavel held by the adjudicator. I would love to stuff it sideways down the neck of those on the other side, but good manners – and the fact that I would be thrown in solitary – preclude me from that course of action.

The fact is, no man can spend his whole life trying to be a tough guy. Sooner or later you've got to try in some small way to behave in some sort of normal manner by talking to normal people – as opposed to cops, robbers and lawyers, who definitely aren't normal.

Joining the prison debating club, and being able to mix with normal people for a few hours every second Friday night, is my small attempt to join the human race. It's the first time in my life I've tried to do something with my head that didn't involve losing ears or teeth. Apart from writing books, of course.

I've never really mixed with squareheads and normal people, even when I was on the outside. I was surrounded by thousands of the buggers, but the only squareheads I ever really spoke to were publicans, barmen, cab drivers and bookies. Oh, and I almost forgot, gunsmiths and the proprietors of gunshops. But to stand with a cup of tea in one hand and a cream cake in the other and chat away to people was never my go. The idea of partaking in the la de da past-time of debating would have been repugnant to me previously.

But here I am 39 years of age – secretary of the bloody debating club. Once, I would have given big odds against me reaching my 40th year, much less having anything to do with debating. In fact, ten years ago I would have put anyone who was a member of a jail debating club 'on the poof', meaning I would have questioned their manhood in a most severe and vigorous manner.

But it's the way it goes. They reckon we change every five years; a fifteen-year-old has different interests from a ten-year-old, and they change again by the time you're 20, and so on up the ladder. I'm a different man than I was at 35. Maybe it's some sort of midlife crisis. Once I used to think I was immortal; now it's suddenly hit me that I'm not. Bloody hell. It's a shock when you approach 40 and find yourself sitting in a prison cell, realising you have spent nearly 20 of those 40 years behind bars. What a waste.

Even as a kid I was always a bit of a backyard philosopher. In those days I always believed that the cornerstone of all correct thinking was that good will conquer evil. But as you get older you learn that evil built the world, and when the so-called great and good men of history wished to achieve great and good things, they did not hesitate to walk over the bodies of millions of people to achieve their ends.

So what is good and what is evil? It's all a psychological blur. When a private individual kills a few people, he or she is a monster. But when a politician kills a few million he goes down in history as a man of great vision. It's easy to see the dark side in every good man you meet, and you can find a good side in every bad man. When you look at history it's been built on a never-ending bloodbath, with the winners claiming the moral high ground.

The losers are always the bad guys, because the winners write the history books.

How did I get onto this? The point is that I think I am changing, or at least mellowing. Maybe I'm turning into that good man with a bit of a dark side instead of a bad man with a good side. I don't know. The difference between good and evil will always be a blur to me, but I am coming to grips with the difference between normal and abnormal, and to date my whole life has been abnormal. So a little normality – such as the debating club – is a welcome change.

Mind you, there's one thing I don't fancy about being secretary of the Spartan Debating Club, as we call it, and that is the title, 'secretary'. The only secretaries I know of got blown away in the Painters and Dockers' wars. It wasn't the healthiest job description. Names like Pat Shannon and 'Putty Nose' Nicholls keep coming to mind.

The Spartan Debating Club or, as I like to call it, the Desperate Debating Club, has been going for more than 20 years in Risdon and does battle with a lot of visiting outside debating teams, clubs and groups. The club pledge is as follows: 'We promise to submit to the discipline of this Spartan Club and to advance its ideals and to enrich its fellowship to defend freedom of speech in the community, and to try at all times to think truly and speak clearly. We promise not to be silent when we should speak.'

The club runs with the full permission of the prison hierarchy – as long as we stay within the rules on what we speak about.

It's a case of come one, come all when the club turns on a show. We even had a family night one Friday, where club members could invite their families along to broaden their minds. In all my years in Pentridge I was never invited to join in on a night like this one. I invited my new fiance Mary-Ann, as she is the closest to family I have got in Hobart.

Dad is 70 now and is not going too well health-wise and no longer likes to travel, so he was a scratching. And of course my Mum and my sister, my niece and my two nephews have nothing to do with me, as I am a terrible sinner. I am sure God will reward them richly for their Christianity when they get to heaven.

I had to take part in a debate on the proposition 'That women should be returned to the kitchen'. I argued that of course women should be the queens of the kitchen. Your bib and brace women's liberation types would disagree, but I think they haven't thought it through the way I have. I believe that men should not be allowed to assist in the preparation of any food for health reasons.

Now, men don't like to talk about it, but they all have one thing in common when it comes to the kitchen: they all end up pissing in the sink. There is not a man living who has not at one time or another pissed in the kitchen sink.

They may come home late at night and just flop it out for a leak because they can't be bothered walking all the way to the dunny. They never tell the women folk that they do it. It is a bit like a dog with the tyres of a car.

I knew a copper once who said his wife was a dirty, lazy bitch. 'I came home after a night on the squirt, had a piss in the sink and there were the dishes from breakfast still sitting there. The slag hadn't got off her arse to wash them,' he said. And a policeman would never tell a lie, especially outside a courtroom.

Ladies, it doesn't matter whether you married a judge, a copper, a public servant or a crook: at some time they have pissed in the sink. I dare you to ask them. If they say 'yes' then they are dirty pigs. If they say 'no' then they're dirty lying pigs.

Of course, it's a known fact that men are usually better cooks – but they blow their nose on the tea towels, never wash their hands after a slash and are health hazards in general. If women could see their husbands, boyfriends and sons when they go away fishing, hunting or drinking they would be shocked.

Men are cunning rats. They pretend to be civilised and domesticated, but underneath that they are slobs. Always have been and always will be. Mind you, most women suspect the truth. And that is that men are like lino tiles … lay them the right way once and you can walk over them forever.

Anyway, my side lost the debate but won the laughs. It was a good night: plenty of photos taken with myself, Mary-Ann, Micky Chatters and his lovely wife, Rhonda, and his young son, my new godson, Zane.

Wouldn't the Lygon Street Mafia choke on their capuccinos if they knew that down here I am THE Godfather. Well, at least to Zane I am.

I am good with kids even though I have got none. Kids seem to like me; there is something about the nickname 'Chopper' they like. It is a word they can play with, breaking it down to 'Chop' or 'Chop Chop' or 'Choppy' and, in the case of one three-year-old, 'Chippy Choppy'.

All very cute and ha ha comic except when their Mums and Dads feel they, too, can take similar liberties, the cheeky buggers. I would hate to see some of these kids as orphans.

IF I have to be in prison, Risdon is the jail to be in. It may not be a holiday camp but the lack of drugs and would-be gangsters makes it bearable. It is hard to explain but while you are in jail and your guts are being eaten out by the boredom, you can still have a good time occasionally. The crooks who do time well are those who learn to have a laugh, have a good time when they can and not dwell on the bad times.

HAPPINESS IS A WARM GUN

I do time easier than most because I've learned to go with the flow. I observe people and learn to find the best in them. Those who fight jail end up being destroyed by it.

On the debate night Jamie Hosking invited his sister and brother-in-law. His brother-in-law is 'Scotty' Neil, one of the founding members of the Outlaws Motorcycle Club in Tasmania, so a chance was taken to clear the air on many points of interest. There was an understandable bitterness on my part toward the Outlaws because their former president gave Crown evidence against me while the Outlaws appeared to me to sit back and not lift a finger to stop him. However, they reckoned there was little or nothing they could do beyond 'efforts' on their part to stop him. What those efforts were I don't know.

Also there were rumors that members of the club were plotting to do me harm. I am now told that the rumors were totally false. The former president, 'Never Tell A Lie' Sid, is now an outcast unwelcome in any Outlaws clubhouse in Australia or America, and after a falling-out between him and former best friend and right hand man, 'Black Uhlans Larry', he is no longer welcome in any Black Uhlans clubhouse in Australia. Or so I'm told.

I can't say I'm broken hearted that Sid and his glamorous young bride are no longer together – the ink hardly dry on the marriage certificate when she left him, or he left her, depending on who tells the story.

According to rumor, Sid is now involved in an area of work that, to put it politely, I do not agree with. All in all, his life, according to Scotty Neil, is not filled with joy.

Dennis Carr told me a while ago that he saw Sid in the company of members of the Satan's Riders Motorcycle Club at a well-known hotel in Launceston. However, Sid vanished before appropriate action could be taken. Evidently he travels between Melbourne and Launceston with great regularity.

Trent Anthony, my former driver, who chose to give evidence against me at my trial, is living in Launceston.

Now, I am sure that at one point Trent was telling people he needed a new identity to protect himself from the Big Bad Chopper. Poor dim Trent would think he'd be safe in a fake moustache out of a cereal packet and an old plastic Beatle wig. Mind you, personally I think it would be an improvement.

The point is that Tasmanians on the run never run far. If they move two streets they reckon they should get a new passport. They start going to a new local pub and they think it's the biggest adventure since Neil Armstrong did the moonwalk. They go a different way to work and they want to throw out breadcrumbs so they can follow them home at night.

Anyway, all in all, the Spartan Debating Club's family night was a good night indeed, and not just because of the debating. Families, that's what it's all about. I just wish I had one.

AFTER the mass-debate we doubled up a week later for another animated discussion with the Spartan Debating Club.

I had to give another impromptu speech. Normally I leave my best speaking to address those 12 good people on the jury benches. But this time I joined in the fun and spoke about gun control and the belief that the police are behind a nationwide plot to disarm the general population.

I am a firm believer in 'one man, one gun'. The state police and the Federal Police outnumber the Australian infantry, yet if Australia was invaded by a conquering army the nation's police forces would not rise to defend an unarmed and defenceless Australian people.

The only way the coppers of today would fight back against invaders would be if hordes of armed Indonesian troops raided the respective states' police clubs and tried to interrupt some serious beer drinking and then tried to jump the queue to order steak sandwiches.

The police are not an army of defence or attack. They are a civil force held in place to maintain civil law and order and to protect property and lives. The protection of lives does not extend to the protection of lives against an invading army. The police and all public service departments remain in place to serve whoever takes control. It is not their job or role to decide which government that is. The coppers have been trained to follow the instructions of the governments of the day, whether the Prime Minister is Australian, Irish or Japanese.

Imagine leaving the fate of the nation to a few fat detectives from the fraud squad. What would they do? Throw their calculators and cheese and Vegemite sandwiches at the invading hordes. Do me a very large favour, please.

There are a few coppers with a heap of dash, but they are supposed to follow the rules and wouldn't be much good in an invasion. Except the Victorian police, maybe, who are in real good form at the moment, shooting anything that moves. And a few things that don't. (What a brilliant career I could have had if I'd joined the cops instead of the robbers.)

After the debate, in which I believe I gave a best on the ground performance, the president of the Spartan Debating Club, Mick Gill, was telling us over coffee and cake about the 'great escape'.

It was at Bendigo Prison in 1971, the biggest prison escape in Victorian history when Jimmy Colrain, Jimmy Gillespie, Hans Obrenavic, Peter Brown, Billy Nollan and yes, the well-known debater, Mick Gill, broke out of Bendigo Prison. I remember the escape well. I did time with all the blokes concerned at one time or another, but I had forgotten all about Mick Gill being involved in it. It was in my opinion not only the biggest escape in Victorian history but probably Australian prison history. That's if you don't count a few hundred Nips going over the wall at Corowa during World War Two.

I'm told the screws nearly killed some of those blokes when they finally got caught. The story was legendary for years. I was only a teenager at that time and remember talking about the pros and cons of it with Cowboy Johnny and Dave the Jew. It was a big deal back then, on TV every night and in all the newspapers, and the stories relating to it went on for ten years.

I was never a big escaper, preferring to do my time and amuse myself with wars inside the prison walls. The only time I tried to escape it was a disaster, as anybody who's read my first book will know already. It was in B Division in Pentridge, with my best friend at that time, Jimmy Loughnan. We hid in the roof and Jimmy ate and drank all our supplies in a few hours. It was like being locked up with a girl guide on a camping trip.

We were caught after a few hours and I was glad to get back down. Poor Jimmy, he died later in the Jika Jika fire. He was like a brother to me until he betrayed me and helped have me stabbed. But I was still sad when he died.

Most escape plots are hatched out of boredom. Prisoners want something to keep them interested. When you have people spending all their waking hours thinking about something they end up finding an answer. That is why there is no such thing as an escape-proof jail. If the human mind is capable of designing and building it, the human mind is capable of beating it.

IN one Friday night debate we beat the Toastmasters on the topic 'Should David Boon become the next Governor of Tasmania?' I explained that I was already being held at the pleasure of General Sir Phillip Bennett, AC, KBE, DSO, and I didn't really fancy the idea of being held at the pleasure of David Boon, Test cricketer and national drinking identity, even if the only books he has read in the last three years are mine, not counting the racing formguide.

I also explained that the Tasmanian Aboriginal population was wiped out in the name of the Queen's representative, the Governor of the state. And thousands of convicts were tortured, beaten and killed in the name of the Queen's representative. The role of State Governors and of the Governor General in Canberra, I argued, is a relic of the past. One day Australia will wake up and sweep this King Arthur and the Knights of the Round Table rubbish out the door, but even while the Governor rort lasts I doubt that even a lunatic Test cricketer who looks like a Mexican bandit on steroids would put his hand up for the gig.

Boony is a top fella and a man of the people, but I reckon he would look pretty stupid in a top hat. And if you don't believe the bit about him reading my books, cop this. I saw him on television one day hopping off a plane, with a book under his arm, and it wasn't Wisden or a Gideon Bible he'd pinched from a hotel room. It was a copy of *Chopper*. Which proves the boy's not only a handy cricketer, but a superb judge of reading material.

Anyway, the Spartan Debating Club won by two points. However, I understand that my habit of removing my teeth to speak could be a social no no and did not necessarily help our cause, although you never can tell. Maybe it cracks the adjudicator's nerve.

But it's not my teeth that worry me. It's my eyes. I am going to have to seek medical advice about them. They are always sore and playing up on me badly. For years now I have done all my writing by the light of my TV set in the dark.

Now and again I may have the light on, but the light goes off at ten o'clock and I write my letters late at night. Sometimes I am writing my letters at 2 or 3am. As far as my physical wellbeing and health is concerned it is like every bloody thing else: I am my own worst enemy.

We meet all sorts of people on Friday nights at the Spartan Debating Club, from bank managers to local politicians, lawyers, businessmen, and assorted local leading lights from all walks of life. University students and dope-smoking, whacked out greenies. Anything from the raving mad to virgin school girls.

The eastern shore Baptists are my personal favorite. Some of the sheilas they bring in don't look like Baptists to me. Ha ha.

The other day, we had a good 'night out', if you can call it that. The Tasmanian debating union arrived with a bunch of little 'butter wouldn't melt in their mouths' school girls from a top girls' college.

The young ladies proceeded to attack me with bits of paper after the debate, asking for my autograph, which was bloody embarrassing. Some older women acting as their minders started to scold them andcall them away like a worried mother calling an infant child away from something nasty. However, this gaggle of teenagers stuck solid and thrust their bits of paper upon me.

I always feel uncomfortable when anyone asks me for my autograph. I'm not a rock star; I'm a crook who wrote a book, and the psychology of wanting an autograph from me is wanting it for its novelty freak value.

Being seen as a freak from another world is one thing. I can accept that. But people asking me to sign books and bits of paper has never made me very comfortable.

I do it because I don't like to hurt people's feelings, but knowing that my autograph is only wanted for its freak value doesn't sit well and the novelty of writing my name on bits of paper is fast wearing off. I knew coppers who were always very keen to get my signature on records of interview which would have put me in jail for a thousand years.

I just hope none of those cute little girls has a daddy who's a detective.

CHAPTER 3

OUTDOOR SPORTS INSIDE

IN jail when there is a holiday it means we don't have to work, and so we either play or watch sport. My mate Rocky Devine lost a finger playing footy last year and this year his luck seems to be just as good. He had a footy driven into his groin so hard that it semi-paralysed him all down the left side of his body, and there he was hobbling around the prison.

Now, Rocky is one tough fellow, but after his brief affair with a footy in the orchestras he sounded like Tiny Tim singing *Tip Toe Through The Tulips.* He was talking about the next game but no-one expected him to front up. Sure enough, he was on the footy field the following week.

One year he loses a finger, the next he nearly loses the pet ferret. I think he should quit while he's ahead – or still got one.

They're not polished, but the Risdon boys make most VFA sides look like choir boys. Micky Chatters kicked 18 goals and played for three quarters during one game with a busted ankle. Peter Wright nearly tore his kneecap off in another game. Pat Burling got hit so hard he swallowed his false teeth. Fat lips and black eyes and broken noses are commonplace.

Jamie Hosking is a bit of a weapon on the field and a bloody good player. Micky Chatters wants to fight everybody. Big Tony Barron is a top player and does not seem to get hurt a real lot. Every now and again C Yard wins a game but as a rule we lose all the time. I was elected the C Yard union rep which means if the umpire blows his whistle too many times against C Yard it's everybody out. Ha ha.

F Yard wins all the games. D Yard wins a few but F Yard kidnaps all the good players with bribes and has all the umpires on side and when the going really turns against them they pull big Mick Gill in as an umpire, banging yet another nail into the coffin of fair play.

I like to go out and watch the footy. I don't play. I may be criminally insane but I'm not crazy enough for that. When they allow you to take firearms onto the field I am prepared to be drafted. Until then I will stick to the sidelines, watching prison matches that could be made into snuff movies.

The star of the footy field is C Yard's Kimble Symons, who kicks a dozen goals a game with a faulty valve in his heart, meaning he could drop stone dead at any moment. Kimble says as long as he's kicked his dozen goals he does not care if he does drop dead, providing it's in the last quarter. Now there is a boy who has his priorities worked out.

The day we kicked off the prison footy season early in the year, Rocky 'I can be bribed' Devine was acting as umpire, and true to Tassie form the rain came pissing down.

Rocky cleared the field long enough for the boys to run off and pop on their hats and then return to play. Anywhere else you'd either keep playing or give up altogether, but in Tassie they put bloody hats on.

In the afternoon the rain cleared and the sun shone brilliantly and they switched to baseball. I would have given anything to have gotten my hands on a baseball bat in Pentridge. Bloody hell, when I first saw the boys swinging a baseball bat I started to go all agent orange, and get flash backs. Ha ha. I've had a lot of fun with those in my time, but nowhere near a pitcher.

Peter Wright, a pint-sized but tough little crook, nearly took my head off with the bloody ball. If it's not big Tony Barron with the cricket bat, it's Power Pack Pete with the damn baseball bat. Innocent bystanders and onlookers should be issued with helmets.

I have never been all that good at ball sports, with the notable exception of the oldest one of all, I suppose. I'm a natural at that, but play only limited seasons when out of jail.

The jail is sports mad. Every weekend and any day off, two sporting events are held. Cricket, footy, baseball and running events are the most popular. On weekdays at lunch time it's touch football. The crims here are a healthy lot. Playing baseball inside a jail is not considered too risky at Risdon. Neither is almost anything else ... it is the only jail in Australia that has an education course in the correct use of the chainsaw, would you believe?

It's called getting your chainsaw certificate. A lot of these guys are involved in the timber industry when not running riot in the local hotels. It's nothing to meet a chap who has bad facial scars from having his chainsaw flick back on him.

The bloody greenies spike the trees with metal spikes and the timber cutters end up nearly killing themselves. The hatred between the greenies and the timber workers is very, very real. I don't think it is really understood on the mainland. In a way it is a little civil war being played out in tiny Tassie, and it can turn really ugly.

I wouldn't want to be a greenie caught spiking a tree in Tassie. You could end up being turned into wood chips. A mate of mine down here, 'Wally' Walford, has a terrible facial scar from a chainsaw accident after the greenies punched a 2½ foot metal spike through a tree he cut later.

My old mate, Wayne Spratt, or 'Spratty' to one and all, was the first man I had ever met who had hit himself in the head with his own chainsaw and lived to tell the tale, but since then I have realised that it's commonplace down here. Which sort of explains why they can get their chainsaw certificate in prison.

The mind boggles at a chainsaw course being conducted in Pentridge or Long Bay, but it's another world altogether down here. Imagine some of the brain-dead serial killers in Pentridge learning the fine points of your average chainsaw. The blood and bone would have been flying.

Pound for pound, some of the best punch-on artists in Australia come from Tassie. I'm talking about the old-style Aussie punch-on artist, the sort that will punch on with you on Sunday and shake hands with you in the pub on Monday.

Some of the biggest, meanest, wildest bar room brawlers in Tassie would have to come from north-west Tasmania. There is a mining town named Zeehan on the north-west coast, where all the mad bastards do when they're not working is drink piss and fight.

The stand up, toe-to-toe fist fighter is a dying breed in Australia. Tasmania and the Northern Territory are probably the last two strongholds left of the genuine knucklemen, and the Territory is slowly being taken over.

There is one very Aussie factor at the Pink Palace that you would not find in any other prison in the country. There are only three wogs in the whole jail, and for once I can play spot the Aussie and win. Yes, the Tassie criminal fraternity is nearly exclusively good old Aussies. Bless their black hearts.

I MUST say I was very pleased when the bloody cricket season finally came to an end. Big Tony Barron is lethal with the bat. The ball rockets toward him from Jamie Hoskings' hand at a good 90 miles per hour and Big Tony swings the bat at a good 100 miles per hour and seems to take evil delight in sending the ball my way at 120 miles per hour. And I'm only a bloomin' spectator. Imagine if I was fielding against him at silly mid-off.

He has nearly taken my head off with the bloody cricket ball on a dozen different occasions. It doesn't matter where I watch the game from, Big Tony seems to be able to pick me out.

It has gotten to the stage where I duck automatically whenever I hear the bat smack the cricket ball. Tony is a giant with not an ounce of fat on him and very powerful. He is fast and a top sportsman and I strongly suspect that the only way anybody could beat him in a fight would be to run him over with a steam roller . . . while he was asleep.

Nevertheless, if the big bugger hits me with that bloody ball I will consult the Yellow Pages under the plant hire section and invest in the steam roller. Having avoided death in 25 years in the underworld, I'm buggered if I'm going to be knocked off by a Kookaburra cricket ball to the back of the cranium.

Tony, the big Fijian, is a jolly-natured gentle giant and a lovable big bugger, and I class him as a friend, but I've shot people for a lot less than hitting me with a cricket ball.

It has reached the stage now whenever he goes into bat I am forced to take cover. I look forward to the footy season, although not because it was ever really my game. The only stab pass I have ever delivered is the stiletto variety. I was once offered ten grand to 'tag' Warwick Capper … but with a pistol. Mind you, the way he's going since the Swans sold him, a .44 slug in the knee would probably have been a good career move. At least he would have had a good excuse for bad form, and a shitload of sympathetic publicity.

Come to think of it, there's an opening here for a good gunman to do strategic wounding of celebrities who can't cut the mustard any more. Think of the press coverage the occasional well-placed bullet would get.

There'd even be a chance of a bit of serious headhunting for record companies with old stars languishing on their books. Imagine it … 'Sorry, old buddy, but the only way we can save your career is to shoot you very dead'. And if you reckon that's the crazy ramblings of a psychopath think about Jimi Hendrix, Janis Joplin, Jim Morrison

and John Lennon and how many records they've sold since they went
to rock'n'roll heaven. Not to mention Marilyn Monroe. She'd be just
another tired old drunk now, if she'd stayed alive.

Anyway, back to footy. The football season is quite a hoot here in
Risdon. It is unique, really, as within the prison walls they play
straight Aussie rules football, whereas the rest of the state plays
Tasmanian rules football. Tasmanian rules is quite an easy game to
play ... instead of using a ball they use their sister and swap ends at
half time. Ha ha.

I NEVER went to boarding school, unless you count the Bluestone
College, but I reckon Risdon runs close in some ways. I mean, they
even have annual Christmas sports, for God's sake. They run the
sports for ten days. This includes weight lifting, football, tennis, table
tennis, cards, scrabble, chess, draughts, darts, quoits, volleyball,
baseball, frisbee tossing, tunnelball, scramble ball, the piggy back
race, the egg and spoon race, target handball, the spit the dummy
contest, the gumboot tossing competition, the chariot race, fireman's
carry, shotput, the sack race, the long kick contest, sack relay, tug of
war, discuss throwing, high jump, long jump, triple jump, the cricket
ball in hats contest, the three-legged race, the iron man event, cricket,
and many and various foot races.

I am writing this out of the official Risdon Prison Christmas sports
magazine, so if you think I'm jesting you are quite wrong. This year
I am seriously considering entering the toss the gumboot competition
and the frisbee tossing. It sounds a giggle. Mind you, none of the
above are really my areas of excellence.

Now, if they had a shoot a drug dealer in the eye competition, I am
sure I would win the gold. And while talking of such manly sports,
this jail doesn't even have a boxing ring, gloves or head guards,
which I think is a bit la de da.

A prison without a boxing ring is a bit unfair on the inmates. In
my opinion it is a lightning fast way to separate who is who in front

of everybody in three minutes flat, and is a true and healthy outlet for normal aggression, and the mental and emotional frustration that builds up in the minds and hearts of men in prison.

Down here, the most aggressive sport is footy, and they get pretty fair dinkum about it. There is even a North versus South competition. The inmates from the South of Tasmania play the prisoners from the North of Tasmania.

Anyway it's all rock'n'roll at Risdon at Christmas time, with a party and so forth and so on. Mind you, most of this hi jinx goes on in the bloody rain because it rains cats and dogs for a lot of the time. Speaking of cats and dogs, E Yard is invited to join in on all this. Child killers, child tamperers, sexual perverts, molesters and assorted sinners against small children are invited with open arms. All is forgiven due to the Christmas spirit.

What a disgrace and a total shower of shit it all is. Being a dog in Risdon is no great problem providing you have a few mates. Then again, the modern day Australian prison system is all going the same way, so I shouldn't point this place out for special attention. Even in Pentridge and Long Bay, if you are a police informer or an offender against small children, you can buy yourself all the friends and supporters you want with a gram of heroin. Not like the old days when a child molester could look forward to having a mop inserted in his bottom and then be flogged to within an inch of his pathetic life.

So piss on them all. It's better for a bloke like me to just shut up and mind his own business. I may as well face facts and cop it sweet, but is is a sad thing to have to sit and watch.

Police informers, crown witnesses, child killers and molesters openly running about the jails of the nation without a care in the world, and some of them swaggering about like gangsters ... it's enough to make you sick.

The Australian criminal world both inside and outside prison is changing fast. In the midst of this trash I find a few diamonds now and again in the form of good, hard, solid staunch blokes, and if you have to wade through a river of vomit to find a gem then it is worth it.

I have found a few diamonds in the Pink Palace, but in general as I say, the whole scene is very, very sad to watch, both in Tassie and on the mainland. The lions and tigers have all gone home to watch telly and the mice have taken over the zoo.

'If you cannot kill the one you want then kill the one you are with', as the tattoo on my back says, but those days are gone now. I just sit with my cup of tea and watch the passing parade and smile to myself. Mind you, it's just possible that the occasional child molester could still have an accident. I'm a firm believer that there is a God, and that some of us have to do God's work.

CHAPTER 4

PROS AND CONS AND OTHER CHARACTERS

ONE of my mad mates in Risdon, Micky Chatters, has gone around the corner yet again to N Division, the punishment division, which seems to be his second home.

He is a top bloke, Micky, a solid, staunch friend who sticks fat in a police station. He wouldn't give people up, and is a hard man, but he can be a bit of a handful at times.

I wouldn't call him a nutter but he can certainly be a bit of a desperate and without a doubt he is also a fast, fierce and furious street fighter with a hair trigger temper. It's more a case of the insanity of youth, with his quick temper being his downfall. But the haste and madness of youth mellows with the years. Look at me, you couldn't find a quieter chappie than me these days.

All in all, Micky is a good style of a bloke. He likes to pop around the corner to see our old mate, crazy Ray Sheehan.

Ray came to C Yard after nearly a year around the corner in N Division. He was rushed off to see his dying father and got only a short visit with him just before he died, which was a bit sad.

Me and crazy Ray are waxers. How do I explain the meaning of the word 'waxer'? It is a mainland old-time jailhouse slang expression, meaning something like: 'I've got the sugar, you've got the coffee, so let's join forces for a cuppa.'

We share our canteen goodies so we both have plenty. If he is short, I help him; if I am short, he helps me. Waxing is a common term in Pentridge, but not used in Risdon. In Tassie the waxing normally involves someone's sister.

Old Ray is a truly tough, hard old crim. He is in his late 50s and as fit as a fiddle and strong as a bull. Poor Ray spat the dummy over having his computer taken from him and went around the corner. Then there was an argument over his moustache.

Ray has about five years to do over an armed robbery and will probably do all of it in N Division. I've known old Ray for at least 20 years. He is one truly staunch old crook who has never given an inch in all the years I've known him, but cheerful and happy to be around.

I worry about Ray's health around in N Division. In the winter weather it's murder in there, especially at his age, poor bugger. But again I digress. Micky Chatters asked me if I would be godfather to his young son, Zane, and I agreed, so I have another godchild.

So the boy and I are almost related, a bit like in-laws. He is Zane and I am In-Zane.

The first time I ever went godfather was to Robert Lochrie's baby daughter, Bianca. Young Bianca is now a grown-up young lady and calls me Uncle Chopper. She's a beautiful kid.

On my wall I have a photo collection that I call the dirty dozen, photos of 12 female friends who all put together to make the driving force behind the letter-writing protest to the Governor of Tasmania.

My little mate Greg Hutt, known to one and all as 'Buck' or 'Bucky', likes to come and perve on my photo collection and make comic remarks. In my opinion he is probably the funniest bugger in jail.

A young model from NSW named Samantha Hough is his favorite and Bucky stands there and points and says: 'She's all right, Chopper'.

'Yes,' I say, 'She's a good chick,' and I patiently explain how she is one of those behind a letter writing protest campaign to the Governor on my behalf. And Bucky says the same thing every time.

'Well Chop, she'd be writing a few letters of protest if I ever got my hands on her.' Then he toddles off on his merry way with an evil chuckle. Of course, I am sure he is just joking and would be a perfect gentleman outside jail. If only he could stay out once he got there.

One of the other pin-ups is Gloria Kermond, a lady kick boxer from Queensland. Bucky said he wasn't sure if he wanted to plonk her or punch on with her.

Some of Bucky's remarks are a bit crude, but they're comical. He should be on radio. He'd be better looking than some of the blokes that are on it now, not that it matters much on radio, I suppose. Anyway, one day I showed Bucky the photo of Tauree Cleaver, another loyal ally who campaigns for my freedom. I asked him later while standing on the muster line what he thought, and he said: 'Shit, Chopper, you only showed me her photo 23 times. Ha ha.'

Bucky iron-barred a karate expert to death but never lost his sense of humor. He is half my size and twice my strength on the weights. He is quite a weight-lifting toff, but it must be said I'm no longer the lifter I was.

I'm now having bother dead lifting less weight than I used to bench press. The last dead weight I lifted was Sammy the Turk. Oh well, I guess I'll just get a lighter gun when I get out of here. Speaking of Bucky and his comical comments I guess in a crude and uncouth way the great Australian compliment in relation to any women is the one along the lines of 'I wouldn't mind getting into that'. It is the compliment that most men use behind the lady-in-question's back, but few women see it as a compliment. It may not be politically correct any more, but I think it is a good expression.

I wonder if the ladies in question would find it better if men thought they were dog ugly and would prefer to talk naughty with the inflatable variety available in sex shops?

It's all part of the rough-as-guts Aussie humor, the type of comedy that non-Australians don't understand.

I HURT my neck and back in my cell one night while practising standing on my hands. There is a bloke here who is trying to teach me to walk on my hands, a short, thickset bugger with powerful upper body strength. He's only half my size but I wouldn't like to fight the little bastard.

I've always marvelled at people who can walk on their hands and this bloke is quite amazing at it. Up and down the exercise yard, up and down the stairs, balance on one hand – the lot!

Looking at some of the inmates of Risdon I suspect that a few of them have only recently managed to get off all fours, so the sight of one on his hands is quite a surprise.

He has been trying to coach me and I have been a keen student but alas, so far it has been to no avail.

The fall in the cell was quite a tumble. A pile driver onto a hard cell floor does nothing for the cranium, I can tell you. I may end up with a flat head and then I'd look like a Tasmanian's sister.

Warren Oldham, the handstand champ, has been doing it since he was a kid. At 39 years of age I reckon I'm a bit old to be falling on my head in my cell, but coach Warren tells me to press on.

I'm already punch drunk in charge of limited intelligence as it is. Any more of this childish nonsense and I will be crippled as well. My neck will become squashed and I will look like an albino version of the English cricketer, Gladstone Small.

I'm still doing the weights with Bucky's 'once a week for five years' plan. My diet is working well. I've put on five pounds in a week. The bloody scales are wrong, I'm sure of it.

JAIL is full of blokes with plans to beat the system. Big Tony Barron, who's the most Irish Fijian I've ever met, was telling me the other day about his latest scheme to aid in the training of greyhounds and racehorses. It involves attaching a parachute to the animal and galloping it with the animal pulling the parachute along behind.

Tony explained the whole invention to me in all seriousness, and it had a lot of sense and logic to it in an Irish sort of way. Nevertheless, you can't avoid the fact it does involve tying parachutes to horses and dogs, and when you think about that it's hard to keep a straight face.

I think the parachute idea has a lot of merit, but it needs one improvement from Chopper 'Sports Psychologist' Read. While Big Tony is tying parachutes to the greyhounds and racehorses I could take certain trainers and jockeys up in a plane and throw them out without parachutes. It would make the rest try harder.

Tony spends a lot of his time thinking up inventions and likes to tell me of his latest brainwaves. Some of them are very smart and unique ideas. But racehorses and parachutes may not take off. Ha ha.

Tony was also telling me about another brainwave invention . . . the unspillable glass for drunks. Tony thinks up things in his mind and on paper in his cell at night. He has some brilliant and some downright comic ideas, and is a bloody great bloke.

Speaking of characters around the jail, there's a big fella called Pat Burling who's had a lot of trouble with his false teeth. In fact, he has swallowed them a few times, but in the past he just shat them out, pulled them out of the toilet and gave them a wash and back in the mouth. Good roughage, he says.

This time he shat them out and still could not find them. My heart goes out to Pat, but there's no way known I'd put my fist in the toilet bowl to try and locate his much-travelled dentures. Pat is a mad drunk but a good bloke, related to my old friend Big Josh Burling. That's Tassie: everyone either knows everyone or is related.

I swallowed my own top teeth myself years ago. They bloody

nearly killed me going down and it was an uncomfortable experience getting them out the other end.

So the message to all you kiddies is, brush after meals so that you don't end up with false teeth. Because if you do, it can hurt both ends.

I played cricket last week, 2½ hours of standing there like a stale bottle of piss, fielding and trying to avoid being knocked out by a cricket ball that I'm sure was aimed at me on purpose. This week I sat and watched as 12th man. I like being 12th man. I don't know why some of the Test players sook when they end up in that position.

After all, you remain inside for most of the day in airconditioned comfort, come out with the drinks every few hours and get first crack at the lunch. Far better than running around in the heat at the MCG, I would suggest.

Rocky Devine was telling me about a wild bar room punch up in which he had his skull cracked open by a mad lady crashing him over the head with a frozen chicken. Sent to the deck by an angry sheila wielding frozen poultry.

He won the day and kept the offending chook, but it was a humbling experience. Next he will be telling me he got the stuffing knocked out of him by an angry girl scout armed with a snap frozen, free range turkey.

Another time Rocky and his crew, after attending to some serious business one night, returned to find that someone had pinched the getaway car. Ha ha.

We sat in the sun swapping wild yarns for the better part of the afternoon and it wasn't a bad day. Far better than being out on the field risking GBH of the scone from some maniac with a cricket ball. It seems so unfair in prison. You are not allowed to carry a gentleman's weapon, such as a shiv, but one is allowed to have the bad manners to hurl a hard object, to wit, a ball, at the cranium of another chappie down the length of a cricket pitch.

Mick Chatters was poncing about in a pair of high camp sunglasses that made him look like the late American rock singer Janis Joplin, only with bigger breasts. He can be a funny bugger at times.

Tony Boros was also in attendance, having landed himself in a bit of bother over hi-jinks with a sawn-off shotgun. He pleaded guilty and Anita Betts got him a rather lightweight seven months jail. Tony's girlfriend is heartbroken, needless to say, but my big mate Spratty is keeping a watchful eye on her as a favor to me. You may recall she is the one whose name and address I swapped for a slow greyhound.

Wayne Spratt is a jolly giant, a former member of the Australian Special Air Service and a Vietnam vet. He is a wood cutter and hit himself in the head with his own chainsaw and lived. Most of the teeth in his head are the ones left there by the saw chain. Spratty is a tough bastard.

I roared laughing the other day over a newspaper article about a plot to kill Julian Knight, the Hoddle Street massacre wimp. The story raved on about Julian telling prison officers of a plot by other inmates to kill him. Well, what sort of secret murder plot is it if the bloody so-called victim knows all about it?

The story went on to say that young Julian at one stage had six female prison officers on a special exercise program and some sort of army diet. I wonder what the name of that diet was ... the Hoddle Street savoury sausage diet? Ha ha.

Knowing the female staff at Pentridge, a sausage diet would be a big winner. In my time at Pentridge there was a frisky prison officer who had half the female staff in the place on a salami diet, if you get my drift. Sort of 'Is Don is Good', except his name wasn't Don. But he must have been good.

Poor old Julian. In between plots to murder him and the dietary demands of female members of staff he must not have had a moment to call his own.

My old friend 'Loxy', Robert Lochrie, is up and about after getting a 22-inch butcher's knife rammed through him. He sat down and had two large whiskies after the fight, then passed out. The funny thing was he actually won the fight, punching ten shades of shit out of the numbnut dago and continued to punch on with a 22-inch blade all the way through him. He's a hard, weatherbeaten old bastard is Loxy.

We all thought he was going to die. Margaret Hamilton, big Margaret, a good and close mutual friend, rang the prison in panic and tears but all is well now and old Loxy is up and about, and making a nuisance of himself in public houses yet again.

Margaret is a lovely lady. I once toyed with the idea of marrying big blonde Margaret, but that, as they say in the classics, is another story. I always make it a rule not to marry anyone I don't think I could beat in a fight.

Present circumstances apart, of course, I generally toy with the idea of marriage after the fifth whisky, and forget the whole frightening thought after the seventh. But in big Margaret's defence I was stone cold sober at the time I considered proposing. It didn't happen, but we are solid friends and will remain so. Now my heart belongs to the lovely Mary-Ann, the Richmond farmer's daughter.

The 'drug' scene in here is not exactly out of *Miami Vice*. A bloke went around the corner to the punishment section the other day for trafficking in garlic! Not that you can blame the authorities for throwing the book at him: half the jail is reeking like the back streets of Sicily. Big Tony Barron gets on the prison video and tells everyone his health tips: drink more water, garlic is good for the blood, eat more roughage and so on. He spent a solid hour a while ago lecturing me on the benefits of drinking plenty of water to flush out the system. I now drink four litres a night – then I wake up six times a night to take a leak. Bloody Tony Barron and his ratty health tips will be the death of me.

I was mucking about with Bucky one day and he ripped a short sharp left upper cut into my ribs. Now when I laugh or cough I get a pain in my left side. I think the little pipsqueak broke one of my ribs. I think I'll have to put some butter on him and stuff him in the toaster. He is a strong little monkey, half my size and twice my strength. Never fear, I'm plotting revenge of high comedy.

I RECEIVED a letter was from a young mate of mine in Pentridge, David 'Macca' McPherson, who wrote to tell me that an old enemy of mine, named Richard Victor Maladnich, spoke to the Truth newspaper a short while ago and called me unkind names.

Poor Richard. The last time I saw him was in H Division, Pentridge. He had fallen over and hit his head rather savagely on a sharp heavy instrument and was pissing blood at a fast and furious rate of knots.

I don't know if it was an accident or if poor Richard was the victim of terrible foul play. Nevertheless, Richard is not a man who tells on people in police stations, so if he was attacked his attacker went unpunished. Richard has had a long running battle with the needle and his personality has taken a dive as a result.

For the life of me I don't understand why he dislikes me so much. That accidental tap on the skull must have affected his state of mind and I am shocked and somewhat hurt that he could express any sort of ill will toward me.

I will mention the dear boy in my prayers. Ha ha.

WHENEVER I've appeared in court in Tassie in the past, big Bill Watson has always been in attendance. He is a big 20-stone scallywag who has been a true and loyal friend to me. Whenever I walked into the court room there was Big Bill smiling at me. But when I went to court for the appeal against this sentence I noticed that the big fella was nowhere to be seen. I asked Anita Betts and my barrister, Michael Hodgman QC, if they had seen my old mate, and this is the story I got. It seems that Big Billy showed up wearing a bandana tied around his head like some half-crazy pirate of old, and they both asked him not to come into the courtroom as his appearance in court might upset their honors.

They told him that I asked for him not to come in because I knew he wouldn't do anything to hurt my appeal, and he waited outside the courthouse. Of course, I gave no such instructions to either Anita Betts or Michael Hodgman. They told me about it after the event. I told them I agreed with them but I thought it was the height of petty mindedness. Nevertheless, they are my lawyers, and I pay them every dollar I have to be petty minded in my interests. That's why they've got Mercedes Benzs and I'm in jail.

Now I am told that my dear old friend Big Bill 'has cancer' and losing his hair due to the medical treatment he is receiving, hence the bandana. Anita knew this before the court appearance but did not tell me until later.

It is a small thing and Big Bill didn't mind and Anita didn't want to upset me, but to think that my old mate, who could be dying of bloody cancer, was told by my own lawyers not to come inside and so went out and sat on the steps waiting to hear the result, makes me a bit sad. He was told that Chopper didn't want him to come in, and that breaks my heart, or what's left of it.

I can be accused of many things, but letting a mate down is not one of them. Who gives a flying shit about the judges not liking the wild look of my bandana-wearing friend. Bloody hell, Anita and Michael said to me, 'we thought it best to ask Bill Watson to wait outside, he looks a bit wild in his bandana.' They jested about him looking like a Mexican bandit.

It's no-one's fault. Anita and Michael had my interests to protect. Big Bill understood perfectly, but the vision of my sick friend in his bandana sitting on the court steps thinking I said not to come in haunts me.

CHAPTER 5

DAVE THE JEW ON THE COUCH

AFTER nearly 25 years of psychological and psychiatric examinations and treatment at the hands of the guesswork gurus of medical science, as well being on and off various medications, my old and dear friend Dave the Jew has recently been told that he has been incorrectly treated for a schizophrenic condition that he never suffered from in the first place. According to the latest scientific breakthrough he has simply suffered from a paranoid psychosis brought about from the horror death-camp stories he was told as a child by his various relatives.

In other words, he suffers from a psychopathic personality. Christ, I told him this when he was 16 years old.

We would go to Dave's place for Sunday afternoon tea with his Mum and Dad and assorted 'uncles and aunties', who were not really related to him, but were close friends of the family who had also survived the death camps in Europe.

Dave's 'uncle' Aaron, who survived Belsen with Dave's Dad, would roll up his sleeve and show his tattoo on his left forearm and launch into yet another horror story.

On one occasion Dave said to Uncle Aaron 'tell Mark about the time the SS Officer shot your mother.' The room was full of crying people and Dave was almost out of his mind with hate and rage.

Dave the Jew's Dad walked into the lounge room and said to Aaron, 'he charges $75 per hour'. Aaron looked up and asked who charged $75 per hour and Dave's Dad said 'the psychiatrist we send young David to three times a week. Can't you cheer up for five minutes. You are sending the boy mad.'

But Aaron argued he must be told, that he must know the truth. Dave's Dad got angry. 'We already took care of that. He has been dreaming about Belsen since he was nine years old. Now all he talks about is killing people or revenge and hate.'

It was true. I had heard about 100 different death camp stories from the people I would meet at afternoon tea at Dave's place and I found myself having dreams about the camps, as if I had been there myself.

It had a deep effect on my mental and emotional wellbeing, and if that was happening to me in the space of approximately one year, I dread to think what it was doing to poor Dave's mind. Instead of a bedtime story as a child he would get a death camp story, and dream of Adolf Hitler.

The mothers and fathers who survived the death camps passed on a death-camp psychosis to their children, even if they were born a long time after the war. I listened to those stories for about a year until I could hear no more and found myself dreaming that I was riding the train to one of the death camps. If I was not a well unit when I started going to these tea parties I was positively feral after a year of it, and I wasn't even Jewish. But as one old Jew pointed out: 'Mark, your father is a Freemason. Do you know how many Freemasons the Nazis put to death? Thousands and thousands – and their families.'

In the end I stopped going to Dave's place for Sunday afternoon teas and when I told Dave about the dreams and my reasons for not visiting his home any more his mother came to see me with Dave in tears, and said sorry, and we all ended up in tears together.

She took a small gold star of David and gold chain from around her neck and hung it around my neck and kissed me on both cheeks and said 'Mark, you are my second son.'

Dave's Mum was a beautiful lady and I loved her dearly, but if a year of death camp stories still hang with me today imagine what a whole childhood of horror stories would do to the human mind. The 'death camp psychosis' suffered by the children of the holocaust survivors is a very real thing.

It spun me out. No wonder Dave took a turn for the worse in later life. His childhood left mental scars which will never heal. Any only child listening to that stuff was always going to be in trouble. They said he had to hear it, that he had to be told, but his Dad was right, 'for God's sake let's cheer up a bit.' No wonder there are so many Jewish comedians. It's either laugh or cry. Bloody hell. It still spins me out, just remembering it.

Poor Dave was an intelligent teenager who ended up being probably the best secret hitman in Australia – and a man who liked to 'experiment' on his victims in a way which made even me shiver. He was convinced he was the reincarnation of the American Jewish gangster Bugsy Siegel. Now in times of high unemployment this is not a good thing to put on one's CV. Imagine it. Name: Bugsy Siegel. Occupation: 1930s US Gangster. References: Al Capone, Eliot Ness and Meyer Lansky.

Dave was, and is, a great friend and remains staunch at all times. He was prepared to hop over to Tassie and help a few Crown witnesses in my trial reconsider their points of view, but I asked him to leave well enough alone. Then again, he's on the outside and I'm on the inside. So who's the crazy one?

SPEAKING of Dave the Jew, he was recently talked out of some madcap plan to return to Israel by an old and dear friend of his family in Tel Aviv who spent some months making phone calls to Melbourne trying to explain to Dave that he can't just piss off from the Israeli army the way he did and return years later and expect all to be forgiven. If he goes back and isn't shot he most certainly will finish up in an Israeli military prison.

Dave's idea about returning to Israel was a bit of a worry for me, as I knew it would be the finish of him. But next it seems he wants to get his passport and travel to France and try to enlist in the French Foreign Legion. He was greatly offended when I sent him a message that even the French Foreign Legion would insist on a psychiatric examination. And, besides, he hates the French. Now he wants to come and live with me and Mary-Ann when I get out of jail. Ha ha. I can just see that ... Mary-Ann would go out the back door one day and end up vanishing like a German backpacker.

Poor Dave, I love him. I often think back and see in my mind's eye myself and the Jew sitting beside Squizzy Taylor's grave (born June 29, 1888; died October 26, 1927) talking of the future. The trouble was that we were so hell bent on trying to control our destinies that we both forgot we had no control over our fate.

POEM FOR A FRIEND

When all hope is long forgotten and the world has turned rotten,
And you find yourself alone, with no one left to trust,
And all your love of life has just fallen in the dust,
And you stand and watch your friends as they sit down to dine,
And you hear their laughter ringing, as they sip their wine,
And you find yourself alone, as you walk the streets and weep,
And you go down to the river to ponder your final sleep,
Your death might stop the hurting but it won't win you the war,
Your death gives them the victory, I can tell you that for sure,
Cheer up, my bonny Cabalero, it's no time to whinge and wail,
Even though the winds of life are blowing you a gale,
So mount your pale pony, and together we will ride,
And just remember, brother, I am always on your side.

CHAPTER 6

MY MATES WOULDN'T HURT ANYONE ...

THE rumor mill is still working overtime. If it is to be believed, Mad Micky Marlow, Dennis Carr and Robbie Riley have all teamed up and, armed to the teeth, have made trips to the mainland, all expenses paid by me, in search of 'Never tell a lie' Sid.

Having no success in locating Sid, the tale goes, they returned to Tassie and proceeded to hunt down Trent Anthony. Stories of near hits and close calls are running rampant, with one wild yarn involving Dave the Jew and a car chase. The story goes that when 'Dave' finally forced a car over to the side of the road it contained the wrong person, not Sid at all.

I don't believe this story. Because, let me assure you, Dave rarely gets the wrong person.

Another wild yarn concerns a '$20,000 contract' on both Sid and Anthony, with the Launceston CIB arresting Micky Marlow and Dennis Carr parked outside a police safe house.

Robbie Riley who is, pound for pound, a top-rated street fighter in Tassie and a wild boy generally, was supposed to be involved in a fight with three members of the Outlaw Motorcycle gang trying to protect Sid.

Stories of car chases, shots fired, fist fights and attempted hits allegedly involving my mates from Tassie and the mainland keep cropping up. And, just to keep it balanced, there have been other tall stories about members of the Outlaws motorcycle gang offering money to try to get me killed in jail. No crim in Tassie is so short of money that he wants to commit 'suicide by Chopper', believe me.

There have even been plots to kill my Dad, according to the rumor mongers. Mad Micky Marlow is an old and dear friend but he is now a Dad and he and his lovely wife Kelly have gone bush with their baby daughter. He stays in touch with me and calls in to see my old Dad. Dennis Carr is a young mate and a friend of Micky's, and he also sees my old Dad now and again, but Dennis hardly ever sees Micky these days.

Robbie Riley, the streetfighting man, is a friend of mine and Dennis Carr and Micky Marlow. I was very good friends with Robbie Riley's late brother big Johnny Riley. He was a top Melbourne crook and a very hard man, and very respected in the Melbourne criminal scene. Johnny and I were very good friends in Pentridge, but he got himself stabbed to death outside a pub in Fitzroy in 1981.

Years later I had a fall out with the Turk who did that. But that, as they say in the classics, is another story.

Robbie Riley was in the remand yard with me last year but he is out and about now and living on Flinders Island, and though he is still friends with Dennis Carr and Micky Marlow, he does not mix with them socially.

So how do these insane stories and rumors get started?

I'm so flat broke I've told my lawyers to file an appeal to the High Court of Australia against my sentence. What my lawyers do not know is that I don't have the money at this point to pay them.

All the book royalties from my previous classics have already been spent on high-flying legal eagles. If I had my life over again I would be a lawyer. You make more money with a law book than a blow torch, let me tell you.

The Supreme Court appeal against my sentence broke me so how I could fund the efforts of three men to run around in search of Sid and Trent Anthony is beyond me, even if I wanted to.

What the rumor mongers don't understand is I don't want anything at all to happen to Sid and Trent. If anything happened to either of them it is very doubtful that I would ever be released from prison. How would I look trying to plead to the authorities to release me and meanwhile both my Crown Witnesses are on the missing list. In fact, if either of them caught a cold I would send the chicken soup, made from an old recipe from Dave the Jew's mother.

Micky Marlow suspects that half these mad rumors are started by the police and the other half are started by drunks in pubs. Perhaps some of them are started by drunken police in pubs.

THE most wonderful thing about Tasmania, in my opinion, is that everybody seems to be either related or friends with each other, or friends with a relative or related to a friend.

The whole state seems to be interconnected. My old driver, Trent Anthony, who, along with Sid, went Crown evidence against me and helped to get me this twelfth of never Governor's Pleasure sentence, is in hiding in Tasmania and has been ever since my trial. (Incidentally, it's a great title for a lagging in jail with no release date, isn't it? Governor's Pleasure indeed. I hope it pleases him because it sure as hell pisses me off something shocking.) But back to Trent and his movements. I get reports of him being sighted in Perth then in Launceston. I hope the brain surgeon has joined a frequent flyer's club: he might end up getting a free ticket to a give-ups convention somewhere. It would be great; they could have a big dinner where all the name tags would say 'John Smith'. They could have the dinner in Asia and serve dog, but that would be a bit like cannibalism for someone like Trent.

I got a letter from an old and dear friend of mine called Kay saying that young Trent, along with his good lady wife and new baby, moved into a house in the same street as Kay in Mayfield, Launceston. Which proves that it is impossible to hide in the Apple Isle for long.

Next thing I find Trent's own brother-in-law ends up in C Yard working in the laundry with me. His name is Jamie Young. Jamie's baby sister, Karen, is married to Trent. I knew Karen quite well. She is a lovely kid and far too good for a thing like Trent Anthony, in my humble opinion.

I think Karen would look very fetching in black. I observe this purely as a fashion statement and this should not be misconstrued.

Jamie is also friends with my old mate, Mike Alexander, the former publican of the Clarendon Arms Hotel in Evandale. The Clarendon was the pub where I was supposed to be drinking with Sid shortly before he had his plumbing rearranged with a bullet.

Mike is no longer at the Clarendon Arms but now runs the Bridport Hotel on the north-east coast of Tassie with his mate Dave Kruska. Jamie Young is a fisherman at Bridport and drinks at the Bridport pub. That is, when he's not in jail. It seems Mike Alexander is still a keen punter. In fact, I've heard it said he still thinks a Pimm's Number One Cup is a hurdle at Flemington.

I am not the least bit interested in revenge against Trent Anthony and I told Jamie to pass the message along. If I wanted to reach out from jail and touch Trent on the shoulder – or anywhere else – it would be so easy, but why bother? It seems he lives his life in mindless fear and paranoia, convinced that my secret agents are going to come up through his floorboards any minute.

Paranoia will destroy them all in the end.

CHAPTER 7

GLUTTONY AND THE GOURMET CRIM

I AM without a shadow of a doubt the fastest eater in captivity, bar maybe the odd polar bear in a zoo somewhere. It was the same at Pentridge. No-one finished their meal before me, and not because I went to any special effort, either.

I would create havoc if I was sentenced to death and then had to eat my last meal. I would finish it so fast that the hangman would still be getting the hood out of the boot when I was ready to rock and roll.

I got this skill at eating food with great speed from my dear old Dad who, in his heyday, could polish off a three-course meal in no time flat. He ate like a snake, swallowing things whole and in one gulp.

He would be sipping on his cup of tea having eaten his meal and a second helping while others were about to start on their second course.

My Dad's dinner time rule to me was simple: 'Son, you get in there, get it into you and get out. It is okay for the women folk to ponce about at the dinner table but men don't dilly dally about.'

After grace was said, I would lift my knife and fork and Dad would lift his. We would look at each other and Dad would wink at me and away we'd go. To eat fast yet maintain table manners is a skill. The secret is three chews, then another mouthful, three chews then another mouthful.

It mightn't have looked pretty but, my oath, it was effective. It was constant shovelling of the food and chewing and swallowing all at once with perfect timing. Dad was always six or seven mouthfuls ahead of me and is the only man I've ever known who could finish his food ahead of me or at the same time.

It was a fine family tradition. Okay, it's not likely to win us a family seat in the House of Lords, but it was a bonding thing any rate. Maybe our family crest could be a fork and a front-end loader.

Dad always said that he hated the way the wogs played with their food – a mouthful of this, a mouthful of that, a little conversation, a drink of wine and a nibble of something else, and an hour later the bastards are still piss farting about sitting around the table nibbling away and sipping wine like a pack of old molls.

Dad loathed it. 'I cannot stand the way these bloody dagos play with their food, son. Get in, get it down ya and get out of the bloody place, that's what I reckon,' was my old Dad's wise advice. 'Bloody hell, son. When I was a boy I was lucky to get a decent meal, let alone a bloody hour to eat it.'

When Dave the Jew had dinner with us, Dad and I would finish off and sit and watch Dave as he fiddled about and chewed each mouthful for minutes on end and chatted away.

Dad looked at Dave once across the table and said: 'I'll tell you right now, boy, I don't like a man who plays with his food.' Now, Dave may have been criminally insane but when he looked at my dear old Dad he knew what he had to do.

After that Dave would sit at the table in stone cold silence and do his utmost to match my Dad and me, mouthful for mouthful. We would finish three to four minutes ahead of him but Dad would say: 'Ah, that's what I like to see: a man who enjoys his food. No messing about, get it down ya, son', and he would give Dave a hearty slap on the back. Dad would start to wash the dishes as Dave struggled to finish off his plate.

I have always taken this way of eating for granted. Dad and me would resemble a couple of giant blue whales going through a school of krill. Just go past the food and suck it in. It's only when I eat in company that people say I eat fast. 'Don't you swallow, you just seem to shovel it down your neck,' they say. Yet I say with all modesty that I do so with perfect decorum.

I can shovel down steak, eggs, sausages, mushrooms and mixed vegies and sweets in under three minutes with total propriety. I have perfect manners. I eat like Prince Charles would if he was on Angel Dust.

I would challenge anyone in a speed-eating contest. I can do it and maintain good manners. The other night I ate my main meal of meat, potato, gravy, bread and butter to mop the gravy up and five full bowls of plum duff and custard and I was on my second cup of tea while the others in the yard were still struggling to finish their main meal.

And then Ray Sheehan could not eat his food so I finished off his, gave Peter Wright a helping hand on his and I was still ahead of the rest by minutes. I would have got into the plum duff in a big way but manners precluded it.

I think only Paul Newman in my favorite prison movie, *Cool Hand Luke,* could have challenged me in an eating contest. The way he ate those eggs got me quite hungry. I try to watch my weight inside, but there is hardly any great motivation. It's not as though you have to trim down to slip into your dinner jacket so that you can get out on the tear and impress a few womenfolk.

The art of eating runs in the family. Evidently my grandfather, Alf the Bull, was not a man to fiddle at the dinner table. You may recall that Alf, a World War One veteran, was so strong he could hold the weight of a bale of wool singlehanded.

When I was a kid there was a 'no talking at the table' rule. We sat and we ate and we got the hell out of there, while the women did the dishes. These days people sit and chat and drink and nibble, and piss fart about for the best part of an hour or longer, then call for coffee and extra nibbles and buggerise about for another half hour like a bunch of grannies at a garden party.

When my Dad left my Mum he went to live in a boarding house at 1 Hawksburn Road, South Yarra. For a while I went and lived at the same address to keep him company.

An old Hungarian fellow invited Dad and myself to a Hungarian restaurant in Greville Street, Prahran, for tea one night. The time was set for six o'clock. As I recall Cowboy Johnny Harris, who was not well known as a food critic, was with us. Cowboy only had one rule about food. It had to be dead and he would eat it.

I was carrying a gun, as was my habit. I couldn't dine comfortably unless I was properly dressed. We arrived promptly at six o'clock but the old Hungarian fellow was late, so we sat down and ordered up three giant plates of Hungarian goulash and got stuck in.

'The Cowboy' was not one to mess about and we soon finished and ordered seconds. We had polished that off and were drinking tea when the old Hungarian walked in.

'Hello,' he said. 'You have finished your meal. You start without me.' Dad replied: 'Look sport, you said six o'clock and that's the time we got here so don't go crook at us when you ponce in 20 minutes late.'

The old bloke looked at his watch and said: 'It's only ten minutes past,' but Dad wasn't impressed. 'Ten minutes, 20 minutes, what's the difference? You're still bloody late. You invite us to dinner and ponce in late. Well, we've had ours.'

'No please, do not be cross. We sit, we talk, we have coffee,' he said in a most cultured way. 'Yeah, well, no offence mate,' said my old Dad, 'but that's how the Germans rooted ya. You were too busy sitting talking and having ya bloody coffee.'

With that we got up to leave and the waitress handed Dad the bill.

Dad handed it to the old Hungarian and we walked out. When we got outside it was raining. Dad said: 'Remember that, son. If ya ever need to 'sneak go' a dago, ya can always get the bastards while they are having dinner. The buggers take all day. I can't stand these bastards who play with their food.'

'I agree,' said Cowboy Johnny, which was about as close as he got to being philosophical. He was always in full agreement with anything Dad said. Then Dad cracked wise with one of his pearls of wisdom. 'There are three sorts of people who dilly dally at the dinner table, son … wogs, poofters and members of the Royal family.'

Whenever my maternal Grandfather, a Seventh Day Adventist minister called Pastor George Weslake, visited us my Dad always let it be known he thought old Pastor George was a 'la de da old ponce'. Needless to say, old George dilly-dallied at the dinner table.

Breakfast was a big meal for Grandad. It would take me and Dad three minutes under normal conditions but Grandad would sit and want to enjoy toast, butter, marmalade, Weetbix, brown sugar, hot milk and sliced banana and dates, with sultanas all over it.

Then he would have more toast and marmalade followed by a piping hot toby jug of Milo, and this would go on with the old bloke chattering away like a married magpie for a good hour or more.

My Mother loved Grandad's visits and would sit with my little sister Debbie and enjoy breakfast with him. So what Dad would do is finish his breakfast first, as always, then get up and start to clear the table bit by bit as soon as Grandad used anything.

The old fellow took a knife full of butter to put on his toast; Dad cleared the butter away. Grandad took some marmalade; Dad took the marmalade. Grandad took a bit of toast; Dad removed the toast. Grandad used the brown sugar and hot milk, then Dad cleared it away. This went on until the whole table was empty except for Grandad's bowl of Weetbix and fruit, and Dad was hovering to grab that.

My Mum and sister would sit through this, angry and embarrassed.

I, however, thought Dad's conduct was very funny. As soon as Grandad had finished his bowl, Dad took the empty and gave him his big toby jug of Milo and that was that.

Grandad's hour-long breakfast got cut down to 15 minutes. Dad would sit on the back step and say to me: 'Ya got to watch the old bastard, son. He'll eat us out of house and home. Silly old prick's got one hand on the bible and the other hand on the fridge door.'

I love all types of food, although at times I'm a little wary of your Chinese tucker. You would be, too, if you knew which crims used to be shipped off to a certain dim sim factory where they went on the missing list. It happened so often it became the norm, if you know what I mean.

Now I have been close to many members of the criminal fraternity, but not close enough to eat them with soy sauce and fried rice. Ha (burp) ha.

BREAKFAST, lunch and teatime at Risdon is always a great joy for me. With Ray Sheehan sitting on one side and Peter Wright on the other, the eating is fast and furious, although Peter's table manners leave a great deal to be desired. Ray, on the other hand, likes to give me a verbal running commentary on every move he makes.

'Ah,' says Ray, 'I think I'll have a bit of the old butter on the old potato. Where is the old knife? Pass the salt, Chopper. I think I'll have a cup of the old tea. Bloody hell, these potatoes taste good with a bit of the old butter on them. Gee, this knife is sharp, I'd like to jam it up George Lawler's arse.' As you may gather, gentle reader, Ray doesn't like the Governor, Mr Lawler, and doesn't care who knows it.

And Ray is a bit of a food critic, as well. 'What's this shit?' he asks. 'How can I eat it if I don't know what it is. I'll put a bit of the old butter on that as well.

'Excuse me, boss,' he yells. 'Has the cook shit on my plate? What's this crap?'

'I'll eat it if you don't want it,' says Peter.

Meanwhile, Bucky's sitting at another table and flicks a portion of peanut butter over at Peter Wright. Then it starts. 'Ahh,' says old Ray, 'a bit of the old food fight.' Slop, a spoonful of stew gets sent hurtling across the room.

Warren Oldham stops inspecting his false teeth to let go with several slices of bread like frisbees across the room. Harry the Greek calls for order. 'Turn it up, turn it up,' he cries.

'Shut up, wog,' yells Bucky, as if he's addressing the United Nations. 'You are not a bad bloke, Harry. but you are a bit like a computer. Once in a while you need a bit of information punched into you.'

Laughter erupts and Harry starts air raiding, which he does well. More food flies, more abuse is directed at various ones, and chaos is the result. I sit quietly and eat my meal with Ray, who gives me a lecture on how it does not snow on the planet Mars, with Bucky calling him a senile old goat, saying he saw a TV documentary about us all living on Mars in the near future.

'Well, you would know,' yells Ray. 'You are a bloody Martian, you've got two heads.' The screws call for silence, but to no avail. All the other yards in their mess rooms are in an uproar.

The whole idea is to eat up and get out quick. Harry the Greek spends most of his day muttering and mumbling and air raiding about bloody two-headed Tasmanians, and then being told to sit down or be knocked down, but it's all in jest.

Bucky has a standing joke that before Harry gets out of jail he will stuff him in one of the industrial washing machines down in the laundry where everyone in C Yard works.

The boss of the laundry is a prison industry supervisor named Eddy Fry, or Eddy the Head, as we call him. He enjoys the reputation of running a tight ship and having booked more prisoners than any other member of staff in the prison. A booking means that the prisoner will more than likely be sent around the corner to N

Division. Harry the Greek is Eddy's number one worker. Like all Greeks, Harry loves a day's work. As soon as Harry hits the laundry he goes into work mode, whereas me and Bucky head for the coffee tin and start to make a cuppa.

'I want to see some work out of you two bastards today,' yells Eddy. 'No problem,' yells Bucky, raising his coffee cup in a cheers gesture.

Eddy has a sense of humor in spite of his best efforts to appear otherwise. 'The wog's got it all under control,' yells Bucky.

'You will miss Harry when he goes. This jail needs more Greeks,' yells Eddy. 'Good bloody workers they are.' Harry spits the dummy at all this and starts air raiding and the daily chaos starts.

The whole day is spent in a mixture of work and laughter and friendly abuse of each other. Then up we go for lunch and more chaos. I quite enjoy getting into my cell for some peace and bloody quiet.

Day in and day out the laughter, friendly abuse and scallywag practical jokes continue. As jails go the Pink Palace is in a class of its own.

CHAPTER 8

NO WEDDINGS, PARTIES, ANYTHING

IT'S time a good-looking bloke like me got married, but the powers that be don't see it that way. I applied for permission to marry the lovely Mary-Ann, but this was rejected on March 10, 1994. Governor George Lawler called me into his office. I had already mentioned to him that I wanted to marry and I had the distinct impression that I was given permission. But later they said I was jumping the gun, and that they had only 'recommended' that I could go ahead.

I thought it would only be a matter of some paper work. After all, we are both adults. I don't think I was asking for any great favors. It's not as though I wanted to honeymoon at Christopher Skase's joint in Spain. A small service inside the jail and some hundreds and thousands on bread and butter would have sufficed. But I got a letter from the General Manager of Corrective Services, Big Ben Marris, 'the Prisoner's Friend', telling me permission had been refused.

However, Big Ben said he was willing to consider the request in 12 months time. Basically, it works like this. If I want an extra bit of toast or butter or permission to get a pair of sunglasses sent in, or a gold cross and chain, or a pair of runners or a contact visit, I go to the Governor of the prison. But anything larger than a contact visit and I have to get down on my knees and call on divine intervention as the Governor is powerless to help. He has the power to punish but his power to grant requests is limited.

Things were different in Pentridge. There the Governor has had the power to authorise anything from a striptease show to a boxing match and day leave to Luna Park if he felt so inclined. He was the boss of the jail. The bugger has so much power he could almost have you shot at dawn. But this is not Pentridge. As for the wedding bells, the hand of fate has interfered again. Every time I have ever got within 300 yards of the wedding chapel fate has stuck a spanner in the works.

I have become philosophical about the old hand of fate, particularly when that hand is attached to some arthritic bureaucrat. They are all the same. They are stiffer than a body after six hours in the boot. They are given a teaspoonful of power and they want to swing it round like a baseball bat. Oh well, never mind, it's all part of life's rich tapestry.

A rooster one day, feather duster the next.

GETTING to the stage where I wanted to get married has taken a while. I told Mary-Ann right from the start that all I wanted was a friendship and that not only was love and romance not on the agenda but I had no real understanding of the word 'love', and I certainly did not want to put another lady through the same torment I had put poor Margaret through.

As usual I set forth with the very best of intentions and after I received the shattering news that I had lost my High Court appeal against conviction, I had every clear intention of asking the lovely Mary-Ann to pick up her swag and boot off down the road, but she told me she loved me and had no intention of going away.

I explained to her that it is a stupid and impossible situation, but my protests fell on deaf ears.

She is a wonderful girl from a farming family in Richmond, just outside Hobart. Her grandfather owned six or seven pubs in Hobart but sold them to take up farming, which is a pity, as I always wanted to marry the publican's daughter.

Anyway, I swore I'd never marry in jail. In fact, I swore I'd never marry. I've promised marriage a dozen times over and been able to avoid it on each occasion, but I'm no longer a young man, and someone has to care for me in my dotage.

Mary-Ann first heard of me in London. She had read my book while on holiday and became involved in a heated debate over my good name in a south London pub and swore to come in to see me as soon as she got back to Hobart.

She said she fell in love as soon as she saw me. In all modesty, this is perfectly understandable, as to know me is to love me.

The screws joke with me about marrying into the landed gentry when they see the Jag-driving farmer's daughter come to visit. Ha ha.

Grave digger I may be, but gold digger? Never.

Mary-Ann has no brothers and only one sister and there were various crude jests about Mr Hodge not losing a daughter but gaining a Chopper, and at least I'd have plenty of room down on the farm to bury the bodies. (Memo to all authorities and potential in-laws . . . the bodies bit was a joke).

I think jokes about Mary-Ann and myself are in bad taste because in spite of the comedy I do trust this woman with my life, and at the risk of using that word, I do love her. I have explained to her that I will more than likely break her heart and run rampant amongst the local harlots upon my release, but even that did not deter her.

Mind you, I think that after five minutes of running rampant I'd need the aid of an intensive care unit and a heart specialist. I suspect any rampage throughout the assorted massage parlours and dirty girl centres of the nation upon my release is far fetched, to say the least.

Mary-Ann is very good-natured, loving, loyal, kind, generous, warm and she doesn't nag at me.

Unfortunately Margaret, for all her wonderful qualities, nagged at me without mercy. When she didn't nag at me the bloody dog would nag at me. I would have had GBH of the ears, if I had any.

Sometimes Margaret would stand there nagging and the dog would bark at me in time with the nagging and while I thoroughly deserved it, I'm most pleased Mary-Ann is not of the nagging disposition.

She went to a posh private girls' school and speaks with a slightly la de dah voice which I think is cute. I know it is a bit sad to get married in jail but the truth is I don't want to lose her.

THE 'let's get Chopper out of jail' campaign that started during the year is a tribute to the loyalty of Mary-Ann and all the great and good friends I have in six states.

Mary-Ann got the ball rolling with a small advertisement in the public notice section of the Hobart Mercury newspaper, on December 29, 1993. It went like this:

'Attention, I am in Risdon Prison convicted of a crime I did not commit. I was found guilty by a majority verdict jury decision and sentenced to be held at the Governor's pleasure. If you feel that my conviction was wrong and that my sentence is totally unjust and that I am not a danger to the general public then say so in writing to the Governor of the State of Tasmania, General Sir Phillip Bennett, Government House, Tasmania 7001. Thank you, Mark Brandon 'Chopper' Read'

Mary-Ann comes in to visit me each week. As I say, she is a top chick and loves me dearly but I sometimes worry about dragging her with me through years of pain, visiting me in jail, as I care for her too much to want to see her hurt.

It is a very unhappy situation that does not sit well with me. Mary-Ann is a big buxom beauty and if I wasn't in jail I would pull her on like a wet soapy sock.

She is a happy, cheerful, loving and loyal girl who tells me she entered into the relationship with her eyes wide open. Margaret said the same thing, but no one's eyes are that wide open.

Sometimes, I feel I don't want to be loved by anyone as I then have the tears and pain and sadness of that person hanging on my heart like a dead weight. I carry the guilt of that person's pain on my shoulders.

It is not fair on me or on that person. Prison and passion do not mix. A jail is not the place for hearts and flowers emotions. Mary-Ann, as a rule, comes in to visit me with a shirt or top that shows a reasonable amount of cleavage, while talking to her my eyes are mostly glued to her ample cleavage. Bad manners, I know, but if Mary-Ann don't like it she can bloody well wear a polo neck jumper.

She sends me polaroid snap shots of herself which are quite lovely. I showed one to my little mate Greg Hutt, nick-named Buck. Greg looked at the photo then said: 'Is that the chick that visits you, Chopper? I've seen her. She's a buxom lass. She would walk a mile before she would even notice I was wedged between the cheeks of her bottom. Ha ha.'

The moral of that story is don't ever show your girlfriend's photos to Bucky, but in his rather crude, comical manner he was paying Mary-Ann a compliment. A few more compliments like that and he could end up in the dim sims, like some other people we needn't mention.

Comedy aside, the situation with Mary-Ann bothers me as I don't want another Margaret situation. It is all too painful. I don't want to launch forth into the uncertain future that goes with a 12th of never jail sentence with anyone's broken heart sitting on my shoulder.

For a bloke who has never seen himself as a great romantic, I've certainly walked a pathway in life that's littered with the broken hearts of tearful women.

I once said to Mary-Ann: 'I don't want to get into another relationship and for Christ's sake don't fall in love or you will drown yourself in your own tears.' Prison is no place for love affairs. How it all happens is a puzzle to me.

As I've said before, when I am outside there are few women interested in a man with no ears, but when I am inside there are offers aplenty. A tragedy, when you think about it.

All a bloke like me needs and feels happy with is loving friendships – cheerful, cheeky scallywags who cheer me up. Those are the perfect relationships to have in prison, and thank God I have people like that on my side.

I treasure those friendships, but a love affair is like a Greek tragedy in prison. It is a bitter-sweet adventure into the world of tears and pain. It's a pain you cannot let go and when you do, it hurts even harder.

MARY-ANN asked me if I'd be faithful to her when I get out.

I told Mary-Ann exactly what I told Margaret in 1986, before I got out of Bendigo Prison to join her: 'I'll be faithful to the best of my ability'. Mary-Ann asked the same question Margaret did: 'What do you mean by that?' and my reply was exactly the same. 'I'm a very sexually faithful man'. In a manner of speaking.

Women think you're just pulling their leg when deep down they should know you are a total rat bag. How can any bloke who has been locked up in a cage for a long time be 1000 per cent faithful to any woman?

It's like a dog on a chain. You put the dog on the chain for the night then let him off the chain in the morning and he runs around and around the back yard like a raving nutter.

You lock a man in a cage for a year or two or longer, then let him out, and you're going to be a sad girl if you think he's going to come home and sit in front of the telly with a tinny, 24 hours a day.

When a bloke gets out of jail after a long stay he runs around like a mad rat, drinking all the piss, eating all the food and pinning tails on every donkey, or should I say ass, he can find.

It doesn't mean you don't love the girl you have at home but it's like boiling water and having nowhere for the steam to go. Then one day the lid gets removed and something's got to blow.

It's a bit unrealistic for any woman to come along to any bloke when he is in jail, form a relationship with him then say to him: 'Please be faithful to me when you get out, please stay home, please don't gamble all your money and please don't go falling victim to the wiggling bottoms and fluttering eyelashes of loose women'.

The only thing that will pull me up is middle age and laziness and the fact that I'm no longer in Melbourne with the night clubs and massage parlors.

One of my publishers, John Silvester, came down to visit me a while back. They must serve a nice drop of scotch on the plane, because he certainly looked pissed to me, but regardless of that it was good to see the sly scallywag.

He was telling me of the new rage in Melbourne, table-top dancing, where these exotic dancers get up on tables and dance for you personally, and according to him these chicks all look like they jumped out of the pages of Penthouse or Playboy magazine.

He was telling me about some nightclub called Santa Fe Gold and the gaggle of girlies at that place. My God, can you imagine me in Melbourne now, fresh out of Pentridge and drunk in charge of a hand gun in the middle of that place, especially with the rumors that some of my old enemies from Lygon Street, Carlton, are flat out trying to invest money in the new booming table-top dancing industry.

I wouldn't be able to help myself. It would be like 'High Noon in Dodge City'.

Being faithful all depends on the temptations that await me on my release. I won't be returning to Melbourne, so there will be no dead dagos or kidnapped dancing girls.

Tassie isn't quite the end of the earth and from what I've seen, half the toss up molls in Australia live in Tassie and a bloke fresh out of jail planning on being faithful to his beloved wife or girlfriend is going to be in for a hell of a mental, emotional and moral tug of war.

Anyway, it's a fairy tale debate because the way things are going, by the time I get out of here, a good root and a green apple would probably kill me.

As for being faithful, well I'll certainly put my best foot forward until I shoot myself in it. Lucky for me, Mary-Ann, apart from being good natured and understanding, is also a very realistic women. The truth is, the only person I've ever really been faithful to in my life is myself. Ha ha.

I WILL digress for a moment and answer a question in relation to myself and the fairer sex. All my life since my teenage years I've always had and kept the friendship of females, and I am by no means a romantic or a playboy.

I think the answer is that I always treated ladies like I treated men: with sarcastic disregard, yet blind loyalty when the shit hit the fan. I treat them as mates. Most of the female friends I've had and still have to this day have never been romantically involved with me.

I've put holes in my manners with a fair few of them but, as I keep telling the buggers, what's the use of having mates with tits if you cannot get the buggers to knock the top off it now and again, for Christ's sake?

Females are strange creatures. A good female friend of mine who I went to school with was giving me a lift home one night. I was a bit pissed and I put the hard word on her. She told me off for my bad manners and I said sorry. I then said: 'Lend me $200'. She said: 'Okay' and I took it out of her purse.

I then asked her to drive me to Horne Street, Elsternwick. She said: 'No problem'. About 20 minutes later we pulled up outside and she asked: 'What's this place?' and I said: 'It's the Daily Planet massage parlor' and got out of the car and said goodbye to the lady in question, and I started to walk across the road to the parlor.

She jumped out of the car and yelled at me: 'Mark, come back here at once, get back in the car, get back in right now.' I said: 'What's wrong?' She yelled, 'You snip 200 bucks off me and then get me to drive you to a parlor!'

I said: 'I'll pay you the dough back'. She screamed that the money was not the point. I said: 'well listen, it's your arse or one of theirs.'

She said: 'Okay, hop back in the car'.

I gave the 200 back to her and she dropped her pants, calling me a bastard every inch of the way.

I was at her wedding three months later, and we are still friends today.

I guess the trick to getting away with murder like that with friends and loved ones is that when the same lady was in trouble several years later I put my neck on the chopping block and risked a life sentence in jail to help her out.

THE FARMER'S DAUGHTER

Yes, I said I'd never do it,
So please don't ask me why,
I swore I'd never marry until the day I die,
But in spite of the best advice,
And in the face of common sense,
She grabbed me by the heart,
And so I jumped the farmer's fence,
She's probably worth a million quid at subdivision rates,
But I'll have to ring the wedding bell to crash the farmer's gates,
Yes, the things I've had to do, and not by halves or quarters,
All to win the pretty hand of the Richmond farmer's daughter.

CHAPTER 9

SEX, LIES AND VISITORS

MY bride-to-be, Mary-Ann, came to see me one hot day with the sun shining nicely, and with her 38-inch D cup bosom practically spilling out of this little low-cut white affair. I told her to cover herself. I was wearing my white short pants 'Sportsgirl size 14' and my happiness at seeing her was becoming quite evident.

A man who has been incarcerated for some time will often spring to life with a visit from the fairer sex.

I don't know why, but the conversation turned to sex and the adventures of my youth. Mary-Ann loves my yarns and sits there big-eyed demanding that I regale her with some tall tales and true from the bag full of comic yarns I carry with me wherever I go.

I was a late bloomer sex wise. I didn't actually trouble the scorer until I was 18 years old, although I gave him writer's cramp once I worked out what to do with the bat.

As I've mentioned before, the young lady concerned was a chesty little policeman's daughter. Skinny as a rake, big tits and a Shirley Temple face. Quite gorgeous.

The most embarrassing events of my then somewhat limited and sheltered sex life happened at the age of 19. It was late at night and summer time, and me, Dave the Jew, another chappie and a fellow called Punchy were in the Melbourne Cemetery target shooting or test-firing a home-made silencer that Punchy had made to fit any hand gun at all. It was an ingenious device which involved a ten-inch length of hose, a jam tin and wire wool.

I won't say more than that, as I wouldn't want some kiddies to try it at home, but it worked quite well. There was a wee bit more to it than the length of hose, jam tin and wire wool, but I will leave that topic alone. I'm not one to promote crime.

The bloke whose name I don't want to remember brought his best-looking sister with him. That is, 'best-looking' if a wanton nymphomaniac with bleached blonde hair, black lipstick and eye shadow, and who at night looked like Dracula's girlfriend, is your idea of a good time. Which, at the time, was exactly what I did think. For me, at 19, anything that moved and didn't shave was considered a red hot opportunity.

She had big tits and always wore a short skirt, platform cork-soled shoes and little white bobby socks with a white tee shirt, and a tight cardigan. A real sharpie chick. The dress was held up, or so it appeared, by a set of her Grandad's braces or suspenders. She looked a sight but the sluttish look, dirty girl face, short skirt and big tits were always a winning formula with any red-blooded male aged between 12 and 20. She and her mates were the height of fashion where I came from.

Mind you, she had her standards. She used to claim that she always said no to Abos and policemen, and she was proud of that claim to fame. 'I have never turned it on for a Coon or a copper', she would boast with pride and push her chest out as a sort of challenge, for anyone to prove her wrong. Personally, I always found this attitude a trifle intolerant, not to mention racist, but you could fully understand her attitude to police.

Anyway, I am yet again wandering off the track. Sorry. It was 1974, I was 19, and the girl in question was 17.

To cut a short story even shorter, the winner of the night-time target shooting contest got to plonk the girl, who loved guns and had sneaked over to spy on us. We caught her and as a result she agreed to act as the winning prize. I won the contest, a beer bottle at 20 paces by the light of the full moon, which is not a bad shot with a .38 calibre revolver. I was always a good shot when the pressure was on. Just ask Sammy the Turk. (I forgot, you can't. Poor Sammy is dead, care of a shotgun blast in the left eye at the Bojangles Nightclub carpark. I stood trial for murder over that, but the good sense of the Supreme Court jury accepted my plea of self defence).

Anyway, the girl was five foot six tall and in a five-inch high set of platform soles was almost my height. She stood there with one foot up on a grave and lifted her short skirt, her legs were quite apart in a standing position and no panties were evident. There were a few extra stiffs in the graveyard that night, I can tell you.

She then said: 'Come on Chopper, hurry up'. That was her battle cry, 'hurry up'. It was a bit awkward and bloody embarrassing. I was doing my best not to appear self conscious, but I can tell you I was very nervous.

The girl, bless her soul, was giving me a gentle helping hand and next thing you know it was all over before it even got started. 'Shit,' yelled the lassie, 'all down my bloody leg, you messy bugger!'

God, I felt like a fool. Then her brother made the mistake of laughing at me and yelled: 'You are a bit quick out of the starting gate, Chopper.'

'Ha,' she said, quick as lightning, 'you can talk.' We all looked at the brother. It was dark, but I swear we could all see his face going bright red in the moonlight.

Dave the Jew called the chap in question a dirty bastard then the brother pleaded it only happened once. 'Yeah,' said the girl, 'once a week'. My own sexual embarrassment in the face of my friends was wiped out by the deep, dark family secret that our little mate was plonking his sister. And it wasn't even Tassie, the home of close family ties.

At four foot eleven inches tall he must have stood on a fruit box to do the job, like a fox terrier humping a labrador. 'I'm going to break your jaw,' he said to his sister.

'Yeah, go on and I'll tell Grandad you've been getting up me,' she said.

All in all, it was the most embarrassing sexual night of my then young life, and one I will never forget.

Mary-Ann thought it was the height of good comedy. Most Tasmanian girls think any yarn relating to brothers plonking their sister is funny. Ha ha.

CHAPTER 10

WATCH OUT FOR LIGHT-FINGERED COPS

OF course, not all presents that women give me are of the fleshpot variety. For instance, the lovely Mary-Ann has promised me a Rolex watch for my birthday, bless her little cotton socks. That will be the second posh watch she's given me.

God, I've had some flash watches in my time – thousands and thousands of dollars worth. And where have they all gone? I'll tell you. When one gets arrested, as happens from time to time, one's posh wrist watch always seems to go on the missing list.

I remember getting locked up for drunk and disorderly at the old *(location deleted)* police station. I was wearing a $5000 stolen solid gold wrist watch – and this was back in 1973 when that was a year's wages for anybody who worked, which I didn't. When I went to the front desk to get my property and sign the book and leave, my wrist watch was missing.

My belt, money, rings, wallet and all other personal effects were there, but no watch.

I said: 'Where's my gold watch?' which I thought was a reasonable question under the circumstances. And the old sergeant just looked down at me and said: 'What watch would that be, son?'

I looked down at his wrist, and that old broken-nosed bull was wearing my bloody wrist watch. Ha ha. I often think the police over the years have arrested me for the sole reason of pinching my various wrist watches. Bless their hearts.

Like me, the boys in blue know a wrist watch makes a lovely gift.

My old mate Cowboy Johnny Harris never had a watch until my Dad gave him a lovely old Datex that he'd got back in 1950.

Somewhere along the line, Johnny had heard the expression 'synchronise your watches' and he asked my Dad what it meant and how to do it. And so started the Cowboy's love for the synchronisation of the watch whenever the Surrey Road gang had to go some place or go into street combat, or involve ourselves in any sort of daring.

The Cowboy would stop and say: 'Let's synchronise our wrist watches' and Dave the Jew, Terry the Tank and myself would all have to stand there and set our watches at exactly the same time as each other.

I tried to explain to Johnny that the whole idea of synchronising watches in battle was, for example, if four men had to attack a single target at exactly the same time from four different directions. But because our gang all travelled together and attacked together it didn't matter, I told him. However, the logic of this was lost on poor old Cowboy Johnny, who wasn't a heavy thinker at the best of times. His attitude was that 'Mr Read' had told him how to synchronise watches and by God we would all synchronise our watches . . . three or four times a friggin' night, if need be, to humor our much-loved but simple-minded mate.

Dave the Jew would mutter and mumble under his breath at this nonsense. 'Who was the bright spark who taught Johnny this rubbish?' he would mutter.

'Chopper's Dad,' Johnny would say.

'Yes, that would be right,' Dave would snarl. 'The same man who thought Karl Marx was Groucho's cousin.' The Cowboy would often hear the Jew's mutterings and say to me: 'What's that posh bastard mumbling about?'

'Nothing, nothing,' Dave would say.

But in protest Dave stopped wearing his own watch, so when Johnny stopped to get us to go through the routine of synchronising watches, Dave would show his bare wrist and say he wasn't wearing one.

'That's okay,' the Cowboy would say. 'I'll synchronise mine for you.' It was then that we realised that Johnny was fascinated with the word 'synchronise' and loved fiddling with his watch, and the truth was he didn't really understand what it meant at all.

Poor bugger. He died wearing that bloody watch ... and I kept it as a keepsake until it went missing one night. Where, you ask?

The Russell Street watch house, naturally. Where else?

WHEN the giant American aircraft carrier USS Carl Vinson hit Hobart with its 5500-strong crew, between 3000 and 4000 sailors rampaged through the town on leave each day and night. And ladies from all over the fair state of Tasmania headed for Hobart, their assorted knickers fluttering in the breeze.

It's not the first Yankee ship to hit town. The USS Enterprise visited Hobart in 1976, and nine months after it left about 300 babies were born who shouldn't have been. And by all reports nine months after the Carl Vinson weighs anchor hundreds more will be born – and most of them will be on the dusky side, color wise.

Why is it that whenever the Yankee Doodle Navy hits town – Perth, Melbourne, Sydney, Brisbane, Darwin or Hobart – the Aussie girls drop their pants and head down to the dock. This shit's been going on since the Second World War. And they do love them big, black sailors. At the moment Hobart town looks like 'sale day' on Falconhurst Plantation. The only twist is, all the white Aussie girls are doing the selling, and the black blokes are doing the buying.

Everyone loves a sailor, especially if he's black, about seven feet tall and with a thousand bucks in his pocket. Aussie girls are known by seamen and sailors all over the world as the friendliest of people. Is it any wonder that the Aussie female has an international reputation? I mean, let's be honest, the world over Australian women are known by anyone who sailed the seven seas as the greatest collection of wanton trollops God ever shovelled guts into. No wonder there are so many blokes in jail for killing the bastards.

I remember once I was walking through Melbourne city centre with my girlfriend at the time, Lindy, and she said: 'Oh look, the New Guinea navy's in town'.

I looked at her and said: 'Where?'

She pointed and I peered off into the distance. And, about 3000 yards away, sure enough, there were about six to eight fuzzy wuzzy sailors in white short pants walking towards us. But I couldn't recognise them as being members of the New Guinea navy or any other navy. I said to Lindy: 'How come you're so familiar with the New Guinea bloody navy?'

She said she recognised the uniform. I said: 'What! At 3000 bloody yards, you've got to be kidding.' I mean, what's a bloke to think when his little 18-year-old 'butter wouldn't melt in her mouth' girlfriend can spot the New Guinea navy in the crowds of the city centre at a couple of miles. Lindy assured me that it was all quite harmless. She just recognised the uniform.

I am of the opinion that Aussie girls have a natural, God-given ability to spot black men in sailors' uniforms at any distance at all. I don't know why the Department of Defence didn't use Aussie girls as coast watchers during the war – although, then again, the German navy was all white, and the Japanese navy sailors were noted for being a bit small in the eight-day-clock department, which makes them no use at all to Aussie girls. Australia's international reputation consists of the men all being drunken rednecks, and the women being extremely nimble at dropping their drawers.

SHANI RAE

I was taken by surprise just the other day,
When the postman brought a note from a chick named Shani Rae,
Now as a rule I don't reply to chesty boob tube blondes,
The last one took my wallet in a pub in Moonee Ponds,
But Shani Rae caught my eye with a comic photo she included,
That showed to me the lass concerned was mentally deluded,
She was on her knees in the shot, I had to look again to check,
But sure enough, there she was, with a gentleman down her neck.
Well I was shocked, let me tell you, fit to burst and cry,
And so I took my pen in hand and sent a stiff reply,
'You mad cow' was my reply (these words to her I wrote),
'How dare you write to me with that stuck down your throat!'
Now I know we live in modern times and things are free and easy,
But I thought a photo of that kind was just a wee bit teasy,
It seems the offending photo, in the midst of a drunken shout,
Was the product of a striptease show on a piss-up girls' night out.
Yes, the modern girl of today is not so shy and coy,
Alas, things certainly weren't like that when Chop Chop was a boy

CHAPTER 11

JAIL BARBERS AIN'T WHAT THEY USED TO BE

IN Tasmania homosexuality is against the law, but behind the walls of the Pink Palace you would never know it.

Before I arrived, I am told, the main game played was a game called 'under the table'. A blanket would be placed over the card table and inmates would sit around playing cards while some pretty boy or wayward youth got under the table and under the cover of the blanket proceed to offer oral relief to the card players.

Every yard used to have its own shower area, but these have been turned into weight-lifting areas. A new shower block has been built with a guard looking down from the catwalk above, and guards at the door keeping watch, as the drop-the-soap competitions had been getting totally out of control.

Back in the 60s and 70s and a good part of the 80s, one half of the jail was getting up the other half. Then it all died out in the late 80s and the 90s. However, recent events have awoken the ghosts from a bygone era in the form of two very young, hip-swinging, raving gay boys from Melbourne's Toorak Road, South Yarra. They have been doing short sentences for passing dud cheques while on holiday.

They are called Michael and 'Jade', and they're a pair of pouting pretty boys who look like spoilt school girls. When they came on the scene hard, tough inmates, who hadn't taken a shower since the new shower block was built, suddenly went in for the soap and water with gay abandon. Not only that, but they were brushing their hair, shining their boots, cleaning their teeth and splashing themselves freely with Norsca roll-on deodorant and Menage aftershave, and prancing about the jail as if there were two females present and they were out to win hearts.

Michael and Jade, meanwhile, are skipping about the place like a pair of giggling, spotty-bottomed girls. I am glad to say that my good self and the fellows I knock about with have nothing at all to do with this dreadful state of affairs, apart from viewing the whole thing with a sense of comic disgust.

The two pretty boys are charging a packet of White Ox tobacco, so I am told, for a little bit of comfort. For newcomers they seem to be well stocked with tobacco and canteen items, and neither of them smoke. Young Michael, the private school boy and the upper class toff of the pair, has been made the jail barber, bringing a new meaning to the term head job.

He has an annoying habit of calling me 'Mr Read', as does his friend Jade, the slut of the pair. In Melbourne they both worked as male escorts and have their own business cards, which they hand out freely.

In spite of the fact I am not overly keen on poofters, Michael and Jade don't seem bad kids and love jail life. Michael told me that a particular (not that particular, if you ask me) prison officer has already made advances towards him. 'What should I do?' he purred. 'A lady has no rights at all in prison.'

I had already noticed that the screw in question seems to have a somewhat unhealthy interest in young, effeminate prisoners. It is pathetic. I told Michael to go to the media on the mainland when he gets out and spill the beans about the harassment of a sexual nature he is receiving at the hands of a staff member. 'Oh no,' said Michael, 'my mother would die.'

The whole thing is quite a giggle. Big Tony Barron said to me the other day outside the boys have prostitutes, inside they have substitutes. Ha ha. But not everyone's amused. My mate Bucky's non-stop sarcastic remarks – aimed toward anyone who Bucky feels is showing unhealthy interest in Michael and Jade – have sent a lot of inmates running red-faced for cover.

Michael and Jade asked me if I was writing a fourth book and did I think it would be okay to find room for them in it. I said I was sure I would be able to find room for a pair of poofters like them. Lo and behold, next day Michael skipped up to me and handed me 12 packets of White Ox tobacco. He said, 'you have this, Mr Read. I don't smoke'.

I said: 'Where did all this come from?'

He giggled and replied that he had been a naughty girl, then skipped on his way with a smile like the cat who ate the cream, or something similar. When Michael and Jade say they don't smoke, I guess it all depends on how you look at it. They have been smoking zoobricks ever since they got here. What gets me is that E Yard is the protection yard. All the child molesters, kiddie killers and police informers go in there. By rights the jail authorities can't ask Michael and Jade to go into the 'dogs' yard' just because they are openly homosexual. So they put the two of them in the mainstream where they both conduct themselves in an outrageously camp manner, in front of the prison authorities, for all to see, blowing kisses at everyone in the place from the tea lady to the Governor, so to speak. And all this in a jail in a state where homosexuality is supposedly a crime, if you don't mind.

If homosexuality is a crime in Tasmania how come they don't have a separate area for homosexual men? It seems that outside it is a crime, but in jail in Tasmania it is perfectly legal and accepted. The powers that be allow it or appear to do so. Either that or they're blind. Homosexuality either is a crime or it is not. Risdon Prison, in relation to the homosexual question, is a terribly confused jail indeed.

Day after day I see young Michael tripping his way gaily to work, with his barber clippers in one hand and a bottle of baby oil in the other, and the thought strikes me that it's a very dangerous state of affairs in jail.

Here you have normal heterosexual men who have been locked up and kept away from women for years, then along comes a boy who looks like a girl – in this case two boys who look like two girls. Not only are they quite willing and eager to play the female sex role, but they talk about it afterwards.

Day by day I notice the jail atmosphere change. Jealousy, bitterness, anger, frustration, and embarrassment, with some men ashamed of their own conduct. The Pink Palace is a quiet little prison, but these two jail cats could end up getting themselves badly hurt because of the trouble they stir up just by being there.

On the mainland, homosexual conduct is perfectly legal, yet in prisons there all homosexual female impersonators, drag queens and the like are kept in separate areas from the mainstream, or sent to a separate country prison. Yet here in Tassie, where homosexual conduct is a criminal act against the law, homosexuals are mixing freely in the mainstream, and it will create trouble.

Michael and Jade were only here for a short time and gone before much damage was done, but for the short time they were here they created plenty of trouble. It was only luck no real violence erupted.

They were themselves physically harmless, and quite likeable kids, and even an old poof hater like myself had to laugh at their antics. I find myself quite amused by the whole situation, especially Michael's habit of jokingly referring to one senior male officer as a 'silly old Queen' and another as 'Miss Brighton Beach 1957'. But, while the comedy of it all is a great change of pace, it is still a very dangerous and potentially violent situation. For a while there, I thought I was going to get the job as the jail barber here at Risdon Prison. Big Mick

Gill, the old jail barber, promised me I would be able to take over his old spot. However, Governor George Lawler said no to me and gave it to Michael, the young poof from Toorak Road.

There was a time when the job of jail barber was given to the hardest man in the prison, or one of them. When I first got to Pentridge in the early 1970s, the barber in D Division was Ferdie Thomas. Ferdie stood about five foot ten tall and weighed in at an easy 16 stone, and was at least a pick handle wide across the shoulders. And, believe me, old Ferdie was a very, hard tough man indeed. He had prematurely grey hair and a weatherbeaten, knocked-about face, but he was a happy, cheerful fellow if no-one annoyed him. He was also as hard as steel and as solid and as staunch as they come, a man with a feared reputation. Few men could or would like to stand toe to toe with old Ferdie.

I am glad to say that me and old Ferdie got along very well. I was a young, insane up-and-comer, and I think Ferdie admired my guts or maybe I appealed to his sense of comedy, but we became firm friends.

In later years I introduced Mad Charlie to Ferdie and later Charlie said to me: 'Shit, Chopper, I've heard a lot about him. He's got a big name. Ferdie Thomas is an old time waterfront gangster'.

I said to Charlie: 'What's that supposed to be?'

'I don't know,' said Charlie. 'But it sounds good. Ha ha.'

When Mad Charlie sat in Ferdie's barber's chair for the first time we were all sitting around drinking tea and talking shit, and for a joke Ferdie said to Charlie: 'Now listen, young Charlie, you can have a short back and sides or a broken jaw.'

Charlie looked at me and I winked and smiled, and Mad Charlie said: 'Well, I think I'll have the short back and sides'. And it's probably a good thing he did, because the only choice on Ferdie's menu was short back and sides or a broken jaw. Old Ferdie is still alive and well today and no longer involved in crime, but in his prime he was a force to be considered. A very, very hard man indeed, and one of the few men I respected.

However, the most feared barber in Pentridge Prison was my old friend Gordon 'Sammy' Hutchison. Love him or hate him, in his day no-one could beat him. When Sammy was the H Division barber he didn't worry too much about giving you a choice ... he was just as happy to break your jaw and then give you the haircut.

A lot of so-called heavies hated Sammy, but it was lights out when Sammy started swinging. He had a bad temper and a bloody quick one, even though it was mixed with a fantastic sense of humor.

Sammy had a great many enemies in prison, and sooner or later they all came down the slot to H Division. Once there, they all were ordered to have a haircut, and there was smiling Sammy. If the screws saw the barber kicking the shit out of someone, it was none of their concern.

Yes, Sammy was a very feared man. You would only have to look at him the wrong way and he would bust your cheek bone. He had a bone busting knockout punch with either hand and freak timing. At five foot eight inches tall and 12½ and a half stone he wasn't a big man but he knocked out big men regularly.

Sammy is a close and dear friend. My enemies are his and his are mine. His loyalty over the years was given totally and without question. He is well into his 50s now, closer to 60 than 50, but I would still rather have old Sam backing me in a blue than 100 young toughs.

Sammy was a story teller in H Division. I would sit in his barber's chair and he would regale me with yarns of wild and comic dimensions about various gangsters whose names won't be mentioned here just in case they're appearing in a court somewhere in this wide brown land.

According to Sammy the greatest stand-up fist fighter in Melbourne, the all time greatest pound for pound, was Charlie Wooton's Dad, old 'Inky' Wooton.

According to the stories I have heard, old Inky was a fist-fighting freak with speed and uncanny timing, and a knockout blow in each hand. I loved the yarns about Melbourne's streetfighting legends and the old time gangsters like Freddy 'The Frog' Harrison, Normie Bradshaw, Bobby Rebecca, Jackie Twist and, best of them all in my own humble opinion, Billy 'The Texan' Longley.

Sammy Hutchison knew them all. He used to act as Longley's bodyguard and knew all the yarns. A haircut could take an hour or so with Sammy telling me yarn after yarn.

I loved it and I loved old Sammy. It's a pity that real men, hard men like Ferdie Thomas and Sammy Hutchison, are no longer in charge of the barber's chairs in Pentridge today. They could both give you a good trim, but with me when I said: 'Cut it up to my ears,' they were in deep trouble. Ha, ha.

These days jail barbers are either child molesters or two bob dago heroin dealers, and in Risdon, they're poofters. Yes, the times they are a' changing, all right. I don't wish to be boring by bringing up the name of that sugar plum fairy, Chris 'Rent a Kill' Flannery, who was put on the missing list in Sydney for being a nuisance, and another dead false pretender, Laurie Prendergast, but both of them got sat on their arse in H Division many years ago, after having the foolish bad manners to complain about a Sammy Hutchison haircut.

Old Sammy has punched some large holes in some very big reputations and it's hard for me to mention his name without feeling a touch sentimental. God bless the tough old bastard.

BEFORE young Michael, the effeminate jail barber, got out of prison he came up to see me and said: 'I've come to say goodbye, Uncle Chop Chop'. Blokes have been crippled for less, but as I say, I've mellowed.

As you might have gathered, Michael was the sort of prison barber when, if he asked you if you wanted a blow wave, it was always best to politely decline, not recline. In the beginning he called me Mr Read but with familiarity comes contempt, albeit comic. In Michael's case I asked him to stop calling me Mr Read and he replied that he felt it only fitting, as at 19 years of age he was old enough to be my daughter.

I told him to cut it out so the cheeky bastard took to calling me Uncle Chop Chop, but at a distance of at least 30 yards. His thinking no doubt was that if he was not young enough to be my daughter he could certainly be my niece.

I couldn't help but thinking: 'Is this what happens to the great criminals of this country. Don't we get any respect from our peers, or in this case, our queers?' I suppose there was some gay shearer back in Ned Kelly's time who used to call him Uncle Tin Head.

It's a disgrace.

Anyway, when Michael came up to me to say goodbye he promptly tried to give me some sort of embrace. I pushed him back and he said: 'Can't I have a cuddle goodbye?'

'No, you certainly may not. A manly handshake will suffice.' We shook hands and I was overcome by a momentary wave of kind-heartedness and I put my arm around his shoulder and gave him a bit of a one-armed bear hug and said: 'Take care of yourself, you little poofter. You are not a bad kid even if you are a shirt lifter. At least you don't give people up', and with a hearty pat on the shoulder I bid him farewell and goodbye.

He then ran off to say goodbye to half the population of F Yard and D Yard, leaving many broken hearts behind him. I am proud to say that the boys in C Yard, my yard, did not rate a goodbye, as the little fairy never hit our yard.

Bucky said we were the only yard in the jail that could hold heads high on that small point. Of course, now that the offending item has left the prison, everyone seems to be in denial mode, but I have got a long memory of how the little poofter won quite a few hearts while he was here. The names of each guilty party is on my blackmail, or should I say brownmail, list.

It is probably a good thing he got out when he did as Rocky Devine, a confirmed poof hater, threatened to flush him down the toilet in F Yard, so he went to D Yard. Micky Chatters wanted to kill him had he come to C Yard. And Bucky was going to break his jaw. So, to put it politely, he was wearing out his welcome in spite of the comic value.

The prisoners who were fond of Michael suffered a guilt complex and would not defend his honor, and in my opinion within another month someone would have hurt him badly or some bad trouble would have come of him.

As I have said before, when poofters run free in a prison they either get themselves killed or get someone else killed. Nevertheless, in spite of my own personal phobias and hostile attitudes and old ingrained hatreds, I have to admit young Michael had a happy cheerful nature and good comic value. He had a disarming way about him. His attitude was: 'Yes, I am homosexual. I do not hate you, why do you hate me?' In my 20s I would have kicked the guts out of him, but as I shade 40 I don't mind the little ratbag.

It doesn't make me pro-homosexual, but I guess you could say that I have reached the 'live and let live' way of thinking toward them and for me that is an ultra-radical change of thinking.

I still think that homosexuality is an act against God and nature, but mankind itself has become one giant collective act against God and nature.

With the entire human race dancing on the edge of its own grave, who gives a rat's about a few bottom bandits.

CHAPTER 12

SEX AND THE SINGLE PSYCHOPATH

TO mention the name of one woman and to tell the whole truth about her presents me with the problem of offending other women, and this has been a headache throughout the writing of all my books.

My previous three books have been more 'Kill and Tell' than 'Kiss and Tell' but I think now is the time to set the record straight. How to name a women and retell a story in a way that won't hurt the woman I am with or the man she is with.

As far as females are concerned I am totally schizophrenic. It is like being in a giant lolly shop. There I am happily munching away on a Pollywaffle then someone hands me a Snickers funsize. 'Oh goodie', I say. I am half way through that when someone tosses me a Mars Bar and I am into that. And the next thing you know I am into the liquorice allsorts. Then come the Tim Tams, when all of a sudden I spy the deluxe selection of fruit-flavoured soft-centred assortments. Whacko! I am just about to make a pig of myself when along comes a sales lady with – yes, you guessed it – an all-day sucker.

It's like heaven and hell and I am lost in my own indulgence. When I am running around on the outside, even though my heart may belong to one lady, I can't help sampling whatever's on offer. I also realise that the axe can fall on me at any moment and the 'eat, drink and be merry – for tomorrow I die' mentality takes hold.

A lot of ladies I have mentioned previously and have mentioned in this book are bloody good people who believe in me and my innocence, and have taken my side with letters of protest and support, and I hold them very dear. Ladies like Ally Grant, Jenny Cox, Mandy Maggio, Samantha Hough, Karen Hankey, Desiree Dack, Jackie Watson, Tan Whitby, Raychell McBain, Gloria Kermond, Kelly Russell, Tashliene Howard, Tauree Cleaver, Kerry Griffiths, Margaret Hamilton and Nicole Sutorius. They are but a handful of the ladies who have taken my side, and it's a pity I cannot name them all.

Some of the lovely and loyal ladies on my side are just that – nothing more than loyal pen pals. And some others are chicks I have known for years. But sometimes in the past when I felt that I needed to mention the name of a particular lady, I have had to tone it down a bit for reasons that you might guess. That is, a few have insisted on dropping their knickers for the Chopper in the interests of getting to know me better.

I have not lied, but as a gentleman, I have omitted certain facts which could leave some of my lady friends a tad red-faced. It must be remembered that I have spent a good deal of my adult life inside jail. When one is released from the confines of Her Majesty's Prisons one is somewhat sexually tense.

Have you ever seen the Dambusters movie when the German dams get broken and become a raging torrent? Let me just say, I know how it feels. Rightly or wrongly, I felt that if I was to reveal my relationship with one woman it was more than likely to get me stabbed in the neck with a broken fizzy drink bottle at the hands of another.

The small white lies in relation to females started in the first book due to the fact that the love of my life at that time, Maltese Margaret, would read it. These tactful little omissions continued in the second book, as I did not want to hurt her feelings. I also knew that with her famous Maltese temper I well could have ended up like that American bloke Bobbit, who had his old fella cut off in the middle of the night by his missus.

Now I don't mind that I had my ears hacked off, but the dickie bird stays where it is, if you don't mind. I made that particular point nice and clear back when the late Gary David started taking the Gillette to his private parts in Pentridge.

As well as protecting myself, I must also look after the fairer sex. I have a situation where ladies I would like to mention in relation to particular yarns, have left their wild pasts behind and are now happily married.

They have gone from acting like Linda Lovelace to playing Julie Andrews in *The Sound of Music*. I am sure their loving husbands would not like to be reminded that they once were rather close to the old Chop Chop.

I am unable to retell the full facts of our many adventures for fear of their husbands kicking the shit out of them. I mean, it may not go down too well with me telling the world that so-and-so is a great girl and a wonderful friend, and that in fact the two of us used to do the horizontal Rhumba together.

I could have told some fantastic true tales of blood and guts and wild adventure, but was unable to do so as a particular lady vital to the story is married and would be tossed out a six-storey window by an irate husband if it became known that she once ran around in company that included my good self. This is the trouble with telling true stories about real people. If you don't like the bastards you can go for your life, but if you do like them and list them among your friends you have to keep a low profile when it comes to the full facts.

It has taken me three books before I could mention the name Margaret Hamilton. She has recently ended matters with her third husband and it's now okay to make mention of her. This is the sort of problem I have had to endure.

Quite a few readers have written to me suggesting that they suspected that there was more to this story or that story than I was willing to tell. They are an astute lot. It is true that a fair few of the ladies in my life have at one time or another removed their knickers to accommodate my good self purely in the name of friendship. But so what ... if you can't hump your mates who can you hump?

I have had this problem with females I have mentioned in my first and second and third books. Men seem to have no problem talking about their male friends yet pretend they have no female friends at all, as talking about ladies in their life would offend the lady they are with at the time.

A man's life is made up of a great many adventures, and involves chicks he looks upon as his mates. However, if any man is asked to sit down and retell his adventures in writing it would be full of his friends and enemies of the male gender with one or two molls tossed in for good luck, but the real women in his past would vanish from the story as if they never existed, as to do so would embarrass him or them.

I find this, in its way, quite sad. Some of my best mates are women. Sure, I may have plonked a few of them along the way, but they are essentially good mates. They have remained rock solid when a few of the so-called tough guys of the underworld have caved in as soon as the cops have said 'boo'.

I have had to describe some old mates as pen pals so as not to embarrass them in the eyes of their husbands and family. It is all part of the web you are forced to weave in talking or writing about real people. It is not so much a case of lying but more of not relating the full facts.

Writing about real people and telling true stories means the whole truth cannot always be told. Fiction writers have the luxury of going the whole hog, as their characters are not real people and their books hurt no one.

I notice when other writers shit-can my books or are asked to act as critics in relation to my books, they are always fiction authors.

These people see true life crime as a threat. Maybe because fact is stranger than fiction – sometimes so strange that it is downright hard to believe – they shout and laugh at reality. Or maybe truth is a bit humdrum and ordinary for them. The fiction writer can turn a bullet in the guts into an epic thriller, whereas in reality a slug in the guts is not worth more than a page.

An act of violence, whether a broken glass in the neck, or a bullet in a body, is over in the blink of an eye, and to write about it should not take more than a page or so. That is why I will never be accepted as a proper writer by other writers. I tell it how it is . . . bang, bang, no bullshit, then on to the next story. I have been there, I have done it and for mine you cannot turn a ten-second stabbing into a ten chapter epic. Not unless you are a fiction writer, that is. And I'm a fighter, not a writer. I know about verbals, not verbs. Guns, not grammar.

I AM receiving mail from very hurt and tearful ladies of the night who have all loved reading my books, but were greatly hurt and injured at my remarks in my third book about my feelings toward prostitutes.

I wrote that falling in lust with them was fine but falling in love was foolish, and that should you be unlucky enough to fall in love with a cracker then stab yourself in the back because if you don't 'then little Miss Tragic Magic will do it for you'.

All I can say is this: If something happens nine out of ten times then it becomes the accepted general rule of thumb. And in my own personal experience I've found a slag will betray you nine out of ten times. That is because lies, false pretence and treachery is the rule of law in their world. A prostitute and a coin-in-the-slot public toilet have a lot in common. It's just that the crackers charge a bit more. However, in fairness, there are walking contradictions and exceptions to every rule and I would be the first to agree that nine out of ten means that this rather severe attitude of mine does not apply to ten per cent of the working girl population.

I have an even lower opinion of junkies but I guess in fairness the same nine out of ten rule applies to them as well. Some of the chicks who wrote to me were deeply hurt and for that I am sorry. However, what I originally wrote in my third book stands. Most of them will let you down. Every now and again you will find a working girl who not only sits on a goldmine, but has a heart of gold as well, but she's a rare beast.

It is hard to trust a girl who loves everyone and kisses each man's heart with a different lie on her lips. My problem is that in my youth I had the misfortune to fall under the spell of several ladies of the night and found myself betrayed.

Lies were on the menu for breakfast, lunch and tea. Yet I have known a handful of working girls who were as solid as a rock and stuck staunch, and showed me great loyalty, but in doing so had to betray the men they loved in the name of friendship towards me.

While these same ladies and myself were never at any time romantically involved, it all gets back to exceptions and contradictions. I will say one rather odd thing in relation to the ladies of the oldest profession – they are the only chicks I've met who will betray the men they love to repay a debt of friendship or kindness.

All in all, it is a confusing and complex psychological question, and one thing is for sure: I've never met a prostitute who was not a very, very confused individual.

Receiving mail from heart-broken whores has been the only time that I have sat and had a big think about something that I have written, and it reminded me that there were some Suzie Wongs in my life. Whores who would bend over backwards to show me great kindness and loyalty in the name of friendship, and risk their necks in the process. But even they would be the first to admit they would not trust nine out of ten of their own workmates.

MY old friend Polish Suzie, the girl I spoke of in my last book, wrote to inform me that she has lost 2½ stone, divorced her second husband, sold the massage parlour and everything else and is moving herself and her two daughters to the sunny shores of Spain. As you may recall, Suzie was once a shy little Seventh Day Adventist girl. After she got married she found out about sex and her reaction was: 'How long's this been going on?' Suzie loved it. She went from a Seventh Day Adventist to a Six Times A Nightist.

She made assorted sardonic remarks about my literary ability and went on to accuse my publishers and editors of being drunk in charge of limited intelligence. Ha ha.

She did, however, jog my memory in telling me that May, the half-Chinese, half-Indian cracker who, with Bangkok Tina, used to entertain me years ago, is now working in the fair town of Kalgoorlie. She said Bangkok Tina died of a heroin overdose in Amsterdam.

Polish Suzie plans to live the life of Riley with her Norwegian boyfriend, ten years her junior, in some place called Marbella, Spain. Well, good luck to her.

My adopted little sister, Nicole, the mad little stripper who used to work as a cage dancer at Bojangles Nightclub, until I found out she was only 14 and I put my foot up her backside and sent her home, wrote to tell me she is getting married.

She's a good kid. She used to be as mad as a rabbit but is a fully fledged yuppie now, so that is nice news to hear. I was playing Russian roulette at a party at Nick the Greek's place one night and I was using a .44 magnum revolver. Scottish Steve had his .38 calibre automatic hand gun on the table and little Nicole said: 'Can I play too,' and picked up Scottish Steve's automatic, put it to her head and pulled the trigger.

As you would understand, an automatic is not like a revolver. If it has a bullet in the clip then it will fire if you pull the trigger. But Nicole was lucky. Nothing happened because it wasn't cocked, but it's only dumb luck that she is alive today. She nearly got the ultimate head job. She looked 18 years old with a top body and was a wild little miss, and I must say it was a big shock and a wee bit embarrassing to find out that our pet stripper was a 14-year-old-runaway.

CHAPTER 13

HODGMAN AND THE LETTER-WRITING CAMPAIGN

THE lawyer handling my appeal against sentence to the Supreme Court, Mr Michael Hodgman QC, Liberal MP, was sacked as Cabinet Secretary by the Premier of Tasmania, Mr Ray Groom, on St Valentine's day. Two days later Hodgman announced that he would challenge Ray Groom for the leadership.

All this plus handling my appeal – the mind boggles. Then I turn on the TV to see my lawyer standing in a water fountain fully clothed talking to the gathered media about the political pros and cons of the state Liberal Party and so on, blah, blah, blah.

If Michael could verbally baffle their honors Zeeman, Wright and Crawford the same way that he baffles me whenever I see him on TV, I'll be sweet, that's for sure. He has so much on his plate these days it's a wonder he doesn't get forgetful. But he never forgets to send me a bill on time. It must be his highly trained legal mind.

Then I read in the 'Mercury' newspaper that prisoners detained at the Governor's pleasure will soon be free to apply to the Supreme Court to have their dangerous criminal orders lifted under a proposed new law. The Tasmanian Government plans to give up its power to hold people declared dangerous criminals in prison indefinitely.

The Attorney General, Mr Ron Cornish, said the Government would soon introduce legislation to take the power away from the Executive Government and place it in the hands of the Supreme Court. Under the proposed new law when a judge declares a person to be a dangerous criminal in relation to a violent offence they will set a minimum non-parole period. The non-parole period must be at least half the sentence.

After that, the criminal can apply to the Supreme Court for a review of the order. Mr Cornish said if the judge found a person was no longer a danger to the community and then discharged the dangerous criminal order, the person would continue serving the normal sentence and be released in the usual way on parole or at the end of the sentence.

Personally, I don't know if this new law will help me much considering the attitude of a great many people in power toward my good self.

Time will tell. I don't know whether my appeal will go on because of the proposed new law. I can only sit and wonder if my letter writing protest campaign has played any part in all of this since I lost my High Court appeal against conviction. Friends and supporters from all over Australia and overseas from London to South Africa, have been sending letters of protest to his Excellency the Governor of Tasmania, General Sir Phillip Bennett AC, KBE, DSO.

Every single letter then has to be replied to by the Governor's official secretary, then the letter sent on to the Attorney General, Mr Cornish. I wonder if 'lucky Phil' got on the phone to the Attorney General and said: 'Listen Ron, I am getting a bit jack of this. Governor's Pleasure is all very good and well but I don't want the bugger's friends and relatives, supporters and general well wishers writing me a hundred bloody letters a week'.

Aussie Post must be laughing.

Well I guess I'll never know what happens behind closed doors. But it does seem odd timing just as my letter-writing protest campaign was really getting into its stride they change the rules. What's next, I wonder, a letter-writing campaign to the judge who originally sentenced me? Ha ha. I guess I'll just wait and see how it all goes.

WELL, I went to the Supreme Court to appeal against the severity of my sentence. Michael Hodgman QC, MP, defender of the underdog, the drinking man's friend and all round good fellow, rose to his feet and put forth my case with verbal expertise second to none.

For 2½ hours he proved himself to be the Godfather of all courtroom verb merchants. He isn't called the Mouth from the South for nothing. No offence to anyone else, but I bitterly regret not being able to secure his services from the very beginning.

Damian Bugg, the doyen of Public Prosecutors, of course was in attendance with his ever ready legal offsider, Miss C. J. Geason. I'm told Miss Geason is a sharp legal mind in her own right and when not acting as legal handmaiden to the Director of Public Prosecutions, she prosecutes some cases herself. I see her as a sort of courtroom version of Maid Marian, playing to Damian Bugg's Robin Hood, while poor dear Anita is viewed more as the bride of Frankenstein by her courtroom counterparts, not enjoying a huge degree of popularity because of her toughness in defence.

Michael Hodgman QC, MP, defender of the faith and Liberal Party rock'n'roll star, however, enjoys a high degree of popularity. It's not hard to see why. When he insisted I wear a jacket, shirt and tie, Anita brought me in a lovely jacket and shirt belonging to her husband who, lucky for me, was my size. But Hodgman himself supplied the tie ... an official Liberal party tie. There's a touch of comic genius about a politician cum barrister who does things like that.

I said to Michael before the case started when he came down to the cells to see me: 'Hey, Mick, how did an old knockabout like you ever get into the Liberal Party with that laugh and your scallywag grin?'

He said: 'Ah, well, there you have it,' chuckled to himself and off he went. At that stage of the game their honors Mr Justice Zeeman, Wright and Crawford had reserved their decision. Damian Bugg, I must say, did not perform to his best in my opinion. In fact, one could almost be forgiven for thinking that he'd had quite enough of this whole case, and would just like to see it end.

Regardless of the outcome, the Buggster was not firing on all cylinders in some of his more recent courtroom appearances against my goodself. Even his assistant, little Miss Geason, looked bored and totally disinterested in the proceedings, not like her old self at all. She, as I remember her in past courtroom appearances, always had that fire in the belly look, but on this day she looked as if she had partaken of a large dose of sleeping tablets. Very dozy indeed.

All in all, His Master's Voice Hodgman was the star of the day, with Anita sitting at his side. The whole thing was ripping good theatre, with their honors Mr Justice Zeeman, Wright and Crawford interrupting at regular intervals to argue or ask questions. I always like to see my judges take an interest in proceedings rather than sit in some sort of senile slumber.

My legal team and I had a good chat in the cells afterwards and I enjoyed a light lunch of toasted ham and tomato sandwiches, with plenty of pepper, and a hot coffee. It may not have been five star tucker but for a man of modest tastes like my good self, it went down a treat.

While talking to Anita alone she had her hand on the bars of the holding cell and I took her hand and pulled it through the bars and put the back of her hand to my cheek, then I kissed it and said: 'Thankyou for everything, Anita'.

'We have fought them all the way and you have fought with me every inch of the way,' I said. I had tears in my eyes.

Even if I lose this it ain't over yet but, knock on wood, I might kick a goal this time around. Still, for some strange reason I am unable to properly explain, I believe that I will walk free again. I still do not believe that all is lost. As I said to Michael Hodgman, 'They are saying that I shot Sidney then rushed him to hospital, thus saving his life, then they declared me a dangerous criminal. Well, if what the Crown is saying is to be believed then if you have to be shot by a dangerous criminal then Chopper Read is the dangerous criminal to be shot by. Ha ha.'

Whenever he comes to see me Michael Hodgman looks the very model of a modern major general in his suit and Liberal Party tie. As I've mentioned above, the tie is an absolute fashion must in Tassie. They won't let you into the better parts of town without one, not to mention the golf club, the yacht club, the bowls, gun club, the classic car club, the private gaming room at the casino, the assorted old boys clubs ... and, of course, the more upmarket massage parlors.

Why, I'm told that even members of the Labor Party and Green Party masquerade after dark wearing Liberal Party ties. If you want to live in Hobart unmolested, joining the Liberal Party is a must. And if Michael Hodgman QC, MP can get me out of this, I'll join the bloody Liberal Party myself. I wouldn't be the first disenchanted Labor Party ratbag to go over to the other side. At least the Liberal Party have the good taste not to ponce about the place in bloody Italian suits.

Me and Michael were standing during one break in the court proceeding in front of the welfare office and a very stern lady welfare worker came out and chastised both of us for talking in loud voices and smoking, and told us to take our loud voices and our cigarettes downstairs. Hodgman said in a whisper: 'Who's she?' and I said: 'A welfare worker'. Then I laughed and said: 'She's a feminist academic' and he said: 'My goodness gracious me'.

We then got on to the topic of Mary-Ann, and Michael said 'she's a lovely girl. You have a good one there, my boy. A bloody good scout. A bloody good scout, indeed.' And I said: 'Yeah, Michael. I've always had a lot of luck with women and used cars. Ha ha'. And

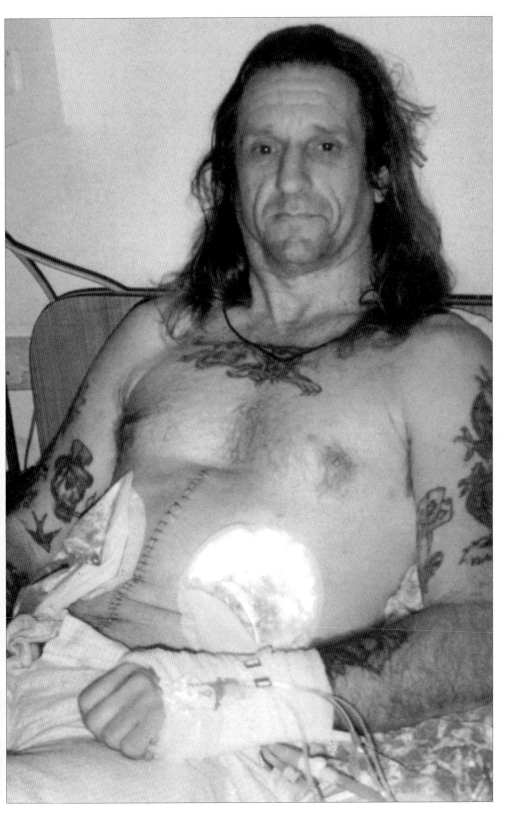

Bobby 'Loxy' Lochrie … stabbed in a brawl but won the fight.

Above: Bobby and our mutual friend Big Margaret Hamilton, checking out the gash.

Below: Me and 'Loxy', Christmas 1974.

Baby shots of me.

Above: I was always handy in the cot.

Below left: I later swapped my trike for the town bike.

Below right: My first stint in solitary.

Thomastown in 1969 …

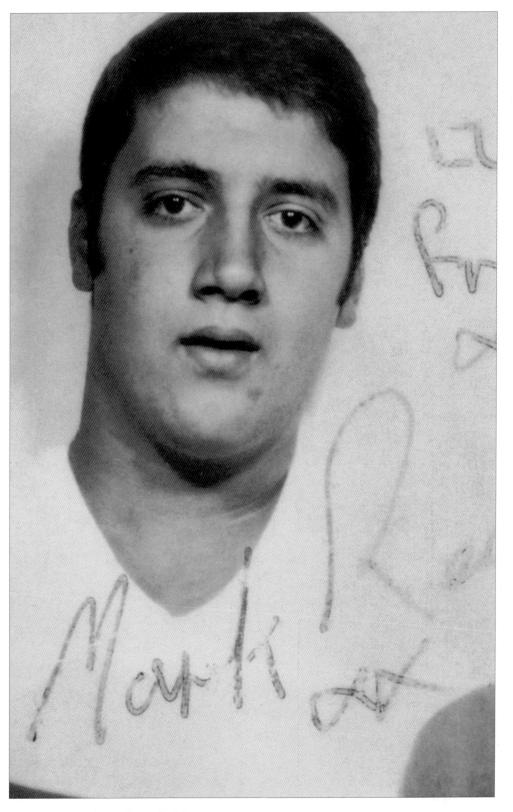

... three years later, I was inside.

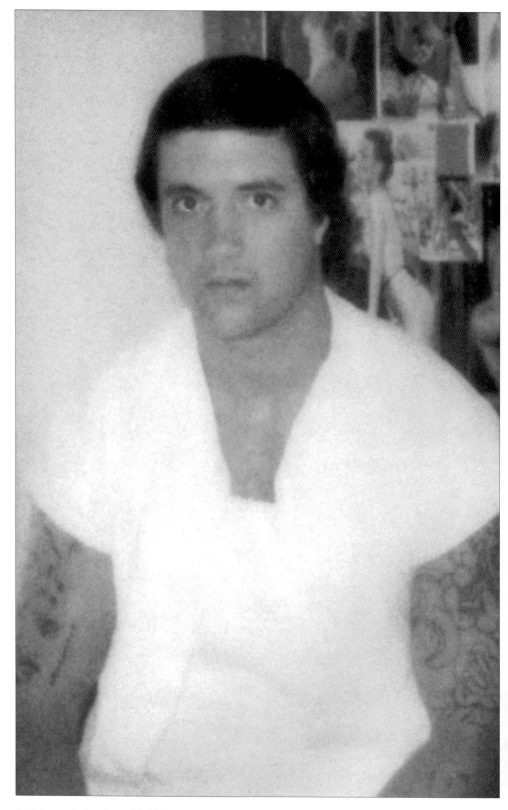

Inside again in the mid-1970s …

… and 20 years later, the story hasn't changed.

Portraits from the inside.

Above: With Jamie Hosking.

Below: With Micky Chatters and Tony Barron.

Above: With Tony Barron and Mick Gill.

Below: With Jamie Hosking again.

Above: The perfect fiancé – loyal, a 38D cup and her grandfather owned seven pubs.

Below: Two boys handy in a blue … Rocky Devine and Big Tony Barron.

Above: With Big Dave Gleeson.

Below: With Micky Chatters and assorted ratbags.

Above: With Michael Hodgman QC, Liberal Party superstar.

Below: With my moustache and my lawyer, Anita Betts.

Above left: Those who tried to keep me out …

Above right: … and Governor Graham Harris, who keeps me in.

Below: Two faces of the Chopper – ready for court and ready for the padded cell.

Me and Pat Burling – he went through a bad patch in a police station.

Above: Rocky, a hard man, but a good friend.

Below: Trent Anthony's brother-in-law, Jamie Young.

Bobby Lochrie with wife number three.

Hodgman cringed and put his finger to his lips and said 'Shush, my boy. If the stern young Miss upstairs hears that tone of conversation she'll have our guts for garters.'

Hodgman is a very polite gentleman of the old school and was very polite and apologetic when the young miss scolded us, yet he has an Aussie rough-as-guts attitude which comes through the pomp and ceremony he seems to be surrounded by. He was telling me that he was a good friend of Mary-Ann's uncle, and I thought to myself: 'Tasmania, you can't escape from it. They are either related to a friend or the friend of a relative. One way or the other everyone seems connected. It makes you wonder about Tasmanian juries, doesn't it? None of the people on my jury was a friend or relative of mine, but it makes me wonder who they were related to or friendly with.'

As for my appeal, Hodgman feels confident. I hate to quote Kylie Minogue, but 'I should be so lucky'. Ha ha. Somehow I don't think so.

A little mate of mine from the old neighborhood of Prahran, born and bred a stone's throw from Surrey Road, Michelle Wilson, recently sent me a photo of herself standing in front of a dilapidated Bojangles Nightclub on the Lower Esplanade in St Kilda.

The joint was closed by the St Kilda Council in 1987 after the killing – self defence shooting death, that is – of Sammy the Turk, Siam Ozerkam. Evidently the place is still closed. One day it might open again, but one thing's for sure: Sammy is going to stay dead.

The odd part is Michelle's photo of herself standing in front of the old rundown joint is about the 50th Bojangles Nightclub photo I have been sent. It seems that people from interstate and overseas who have read my books and who are travelling to Melbourne on holiday, for some strange reason make their way to the old rundown nightclub on the beach and stand in front of it for a snap shot. It is kind of like people travelling to London on holiday and having themselves photographed standing in front of the Blind Beggar Pub in London's East End, where Ronnie Kray did the so-called 'lager and lime' murder.

I don't want to put shit on myself but the shooting of Siam 'Sammy the Turk' Ozerkam outside Bojangles Nightclub in 1987 was probably the most unimportant and non-event murder case in Australian criminal history, and Bojangles was the lowest blood-and-guts dive in Melbourne, but I've received letters and photos from everyone from South African backpackers to international air hostesses who have visited the joint for a souvenir snapshot.

Some people send me photos of themselves standing in on or near the exact spot where Sammy got shot dead. Perhaps me killing that nitwit has been good for the economy. Just think of it as the old Chop Chop doing his bit for tourism in Victoria. Maybe Jeff Kennett could thank me by leaning on his mates down here in Tassie to give me a break. I promise to keep up the good work by spending heaps in his new casino. And I'd keep some of the vermin out of the place.

It is all very strange. When Dave the Jew, Terry the Tank, Cowboy Johnny Harris and myself met for our secret meetings to discuss our teenage battle plans we would often get on the phone and talk in our numb nut code, flattering our stupid selves that the phone was tapped. We'd say something highly secret like 'meet you at Squizzy's place this afternoon, two o'clock'.

This meant we would meet up at the Melbourne Cemetery in Carlton at Squizzy Taylor's grave. This happened half a dozen times and me and the Jew used Squizzy's grave site as a meeting place in 1977 and again in 1987. We would convince ourselves that the phone was off tap or that we were under surveillance, and we would simply ring each other and say meet you at the spot and the time and would meet up at Taylor's grave. Generally it was after dark, which was spooky, as Dave would always get there ahead of me and hide, then sneak up on me from behind. Which shows how mad he is. He could have got himself accidentally shot.

The point of this rave is, has Bojangles now become a meeting point for the mentally ill? The people who used to go there when it was open were not exactly well units, but those who go there now it is closed are clearly unbalanced.

It would be a bit black and spooky loitering around that area after dark, but it seems that for some the old nightclub has become a meeting place, a morbid tourist attraction for the crime buffs or the Chopper Read buffs.

It is a funny old world we live in. I know that Dave the Jew regularly places flowers on Squizzy Taylor's grave and has sat on the front steps of Bojangles nightclub. Poor old Dave gets a bit lonely these days.

THE MEETING PLACE

In the hysteria of our insane minds when facing the Devil's host,
We would go to seek the mystic council of the dead king's ghost,
And the place we always ran to was a silent place to go,
We would speak of secret things that only we would know,
And talk of war and battles and blood feuds yet to fight,
And in our hearts we prayed for a sign that we were right,
Yes, in our madness we would sit and chat, just me and Dave
In the middle of the night, like nuts, beside old Squizzy's grave.

M.B.R.

CHAPTER 14

BOB HAWKE, ROYALTY AND ME

MY lawyer Anita Betts brought Michael Hodgman QC to see me one Saturday and we had a chat for about an hour or so. As I've said, he is the strangest Liberal politician I've ever met and I have met a few of the bastards in my time, around racecourses and other places where sporting gentlemen gather for fun and fancy. Hodgman is very much a fighter for the underdog, a Lt. Commander in the Navy Reserve and rumored to have been a dashing lady's man in his single days.

I ran a little jest past him – about a suave devil like him bringing new meaning to the naval term 'permission to go below' – and he roared laughing. He is the most knockabout Liberal politician I've ever come across, and rates with knockabouts of all sorts.

In my youth my old gunman mate Horatio Morris would take me to the John Curtin Hotel in Lygon Street, Carlton, a pub littered with union leaders, commies, Labor politicians and similar riff raff.

It was a common sight to see Norm Gallagher, then still very much the boss of the Builders' Laborers, drinking with Bob Hawke, the boss of the ACTU. Not to mention John Halfpenny, Laurie Carmichael and assorted Trades Hall backroom heavyweights.

The place was like a second home for a lot of this mob. One night I, together with others, helped Bob Hawke after he had fallen over in the toilet and was very sick. Obviously, he had eaten something which didn't agree with him.

Of course, seeing someone drunk in those days was not uncommon at the John Curtin. After the fifth drink every bugger seemed to turn commie and they started calling each other 'comrade'. I remember once when a member of the Waterside Workers Federation held a member of the Trades Hall Council at gunpoint in the men's toilet over non-payment of a debt and a prominent member of the BLF stepped in and repaid the debt himself, then turned to the bloke from the THC and said: 'That's your vote whenever I need it'. That's politics, I guess, whether it's the Victorian Left or the NSW Right.

As a 17-year-old kid in the company of one of the most feared old time criminal fighters in Melbourne, my presence at the hotel was never questioned. Billy 'the Texan' Longley would make appearances. Pat Shannon, 'Putty Nose' Nicholls, Big Dougy Sproule, football players, TV and newspaper reporters, politicians' wives and professional whores. It was an odd mixture indeed.

Bob Hawke was a strange bloke in those days. I know he got off the piss in later years, but Hawke and his drunken, loud raving voice could be heard all over the bar. How the bloke was never taken outside and kicked senseless is a puzzle. It's a good thing he didn't get down to the police club or a dockies' pub and bung on an act, because he would have had his face re-arranged nice and quick. He was never as popular as he thought he was. He was very powerful, but not loved by those who knew him, which is fair enough and the way it often is.

I've never been a real fan of Hawke's since then. I have always taken my hat off to the work he did but not the man himself. What I want to know now is when we are going to hear the end of him? When he became Prime Minister in 1983, a popular rank and file Labor Party tune was 'The working class can kiss his arse, Bob's got the foreman's job at last'. But every poor mug Labor true believer thought that he was Jack Lang, Doc Evatt and Gough Bloody Whitlam all come again. Didn't Bill Hayden mark him well with his immortal 'drover's dog' remark? The only true Labor prime ministers that Aussie land has had were John Joseph Curtin, 1941-45, and Edward Gough Whitlam, 1972-75.

As for Hawke, as far as I'm concerned and as far as a million other Aussie Labor-voting battlers are concerned, he will always be remembered as the bloke who invited the ALP to the dance, then bent the old moll over and screwed the arse off her. And who was holding Hawke's coat while he did it ... Jack Lang's pet in his dago suit. If Hawke was the drover's dog, then it is fair to say Keating is what the dog left behind.

Like a lot of things in this country, the ALP is a poor imitation of what it once was. I've always been Labor – very Right-wing Labor – but if the shower of shit they are raining down on us now is all they have left to offer, then bugger it, I'll join the bloody Liberal Party.

I think my trouble is that I have become a bit of a sceptical old dinosaur. I've seen too much and I've become jaded and very suspicious. The world is changing and I don't seem to be changing with it. The prison system is no longer the way it was, the criminal world is no longer the one I grew up in, and the police of today do not possess the same sense of poetic justice and black comedy the rough-as-guts old bulls seemed to have when I was a young up and comer. And the Labor Party is no longer the party it once was.

The whole nation is turning gay or green in a vomit of political correctness. Everyone's torn up their Smokey Dawson membership cards and tossed them in the fire, half the country couldn't tell you who Banjo Paterson or Ned Kelly were, and the whole nation is steaming full steam ahead into the 21st century to the electric hip hop beat of some Yankee Doodle basketball music . . . and I'm just walking backwards in the other direction 'back down that track to an old fashioned shack' to the Aussie land of my memory.

Anyway, back to Michael Hodgman, who I left stranded about a page ago. The point of all this is that he had that same old-time feel and personality of a knockabout Trades Hall Council boss, a real true believing red rag Labor man.

A real knockabout fighter for the underdog with none of this old school tie, toffy-nosed Liberal crap about him, he sat in front of me talking about my appeal and I sat there wondering how the hell he got into the Liberal Party. Maybe it is because in some ways his personality is not unlike my own, although I am clearly better looking. Maybe he should be Prime Minister and I could be Treasurer. Anyone who didn't pay their taxes, off with their toes. Putting a few spivs on the missing list would help clear the unemployment rate.

Michael Hodgman can talk the leg off an iron pot, but makes plenty of sense. I felt very confident about him. I want to say that it was disconcerting but it was a bit strange. There I was in a small interview room talking about my legal problems with a man who could quite easily become the next Premier of Tasmania or the Attorney General. I haven't made any rash statements about victory, but I am very happy to have this rough diamond on side. I only wish I had him at my High Court appeal.

I've noticed that the Liberal Party and its political arm are gathering men into its ranks that could have easily gone very well in the Labor Party, and the poor old ALP is becoming more and more effeminate.

One could hardly imagine the Labor Party membership of today breasting the bar of the John Curtin Hotel 20 years ago.

THE Republican debate is really starting to piss me off. I suspect that the whole thing is a Labor Party plot. A case of no food in the fridge so, to take our minds of what really matters, let's repaint the house.

I like the Queen of England and the royal family, although a few of the younger ones could do with a blindfold and a last cigarette. The Queen herself is a lovely old dear, but she is the Queen of England, Scotland, Wales and Northern (in name only) Ireland. She is not the Queen of Aussie land. Well, she is, but no-one really takes it seriously, outside the Melbourne Club.

On the other hand, if we became a republic the Queen would no longer be our head of state, yet we would remain in the Commonwealth, and the Queen is the figurehead of the Commonwealth.

I like the sound of a republic, but our legal and political system is, and will always remain very old school tie and English.

Neither the Liberals nor the Labor party want to give the Australian people a Bill of Rights. Even with all the republican chatter from the Labor Party and his Catholic Holiness, Paul Keating, perish the thought that the Australian public should be given a Bill of Rights.

Mention Bill of Rights and they say we have the constitution to protect us. The same constitution Paul Keating said was drawn up by the British Foreign office as a means to look over our shoulders. So on one hand while I applaud Keating and his efforts, I keep thinking the whole thing is a house painting exercise and that in reality nothing will change. The Governor-General will be replaced with a president, the constitution will be changed hardly at all.

The whole thing needs updating and rewriting. I mean if the old is so bad then replace it with something better, not with something almost as bad. What do the people get? Bugger all. That's what.

Any government that says no to a Bill of Rights should be seriously asked why at the ballot box. A nation that has no Bill of Rights to offer its people believes that the people deserve all the rights in the world except for the ones they don't want them to have.

I mean what is this problem that Aussie pollies have with

introducing a legally binding Bill which states the individual rights of the citizens? At the moment, most people really don't know what they can and can't do. They can be so easily bluffed by authority.

The politicians are really quite frightened by the thought of the general public, the great unwashed, having a clear-cut Bill of Rights that the police, the courts, and the public service could not infringe.

Without such a Bill of Rights, the republic talk is total flap doodle.

But, as always, I strongly suspect that the poor old Aussie will get nothing out of this except for a fireworks display paid for by the taxpayer on the night that a republic is declared. There is no doubt about us Aussies ... for a few free drinks, a party hat and a balloon with a whoopee-doo fireworks display thrown in every now and again, our politicians can get up us whenever they want.

Viva the bloody republic. What a con.

CHAPTER 15

GARY DIED TRYING TO BLUFF ACES WITH A JOKER

ON APRIL 9, 1989, two police from Melbourne's City West police station arrested a minor criminal, Gary Abdallah, and took him back to his flat in inner-suburban Carlton. They had arrested him and were to charge him with attempted murder over an incident where a young man had allegedly been deliberately run over outside a city nightspot.

The two police, Senior Detectives Dermot Avon and Cliff Lockwood, said they went back to the flat to search it for incriminating evidence. Significantly, perhaps, police also believed that Abdallah may have had knowledge about the murder of two police, Constables Steven Tynan and Damian Eyre, who were ambushed in Walsh Street, South Yarra, on October 12, 1988.

Avon and Lockwood claimed that while searching a first storey bedroom of the Drummond Street flat, Abdallah grabbed a firearm and threatened them. Lockwood emptied his .38 calibre service revolver and then grabbed his partner's gun to fire a seventh shot, according to their later testimony.

Police later found the gun the two police said they were threatened *with was an imitation .357 magnum revolver. Abdallah was shot several times, the last bullet smashed into his head. He fell into a coma and died on May 19.*

The two detectives were charged with murder in 1993 in controversial circumstances where they were presented directly for trial and were not given a committal hearing. They were acquitted by a Supreme Court Jury in February, 1994.

Dermot Avon returned to duty but Cliff Lockwood left the force in July, 1994, saying he felt he would always find it difficult to return to street policing as he believed his name would always be unfairly linked to the case.

'I suspect I will always be a marked man,' he said. 'I want to get on with my life. What happened with the Abdallah matter would never go away. Every time I jumped into the witness box, solicitors would be dragging out the same old allegations.'

WELL, the Gary Abdallah murder trial case – fiasco, call it what you will – is over at long last. I had nothing against young Abdallah. He was just a young punk kid with dreams and a small local reputation that one suspects he wanted to turn into a large reputation.

I guess you could say young Gazza was on his way up, but you would need to have a rather broad mind and a good sense of comedy to seriously suggest that his urgent desire to climb the criminal ladder meant that he would ever have got to the top.

If it had not been for his early death, no-one would have heard of him again. But many young up and coming gangsters like him are full of bluff and bullshit, and it seems a lot of them hold this comic idea that if you pull a gun on a copper he will duck, dive and run like hell.

Back in the days when coppers never carried guns and few, if any, criminals ever did, the sight of a firearm would no doubt send the balls running into the underpants, but the Americanisation of the Australian criminal world and police forces in relation to guns has instilled the wild west shoot'em up mentality into both cops and robbers.

Now, if you pull it you had better not be bluffing. There was a case in Launceston in 1993 when a young 16-year-old called Ricky Maynard pulled a replica revolver on two uniformed police and got himself killed.

It's all got to do with the 'bluff' mentality of youth that if you get the drop on them first with a gun, real or otherwise, they will weaken. It is a big bet to place on the table. I've noticed that a lot of young would-be toughs have this bluff and bullshit mentality. I guess that's why I'm one of the few crooks who believe Abdallah did pull out that replica .357 magnum. Why? Because if police were going to waste Abdallah they would have put a real hand gun in his hands after the event, and would have done the job with one or two clear shots.

Seven shots is obviously the result of blind panic, not cold blood and clear thought, and loading a bloke up with a shitpot replica after you have wasted him with seven shots is only turning a simple thing into a bloody nightmare that no-one will believe.

I find it impossible to believe that Lockwood and Avon were incapable, due to lack of connections, of laying their hands on a real handgun or sawn-off shotgun to load up Abdallah, had they wanted to do so.

A real gun in Abdallah's hand and it is case closed, police valor medals and free drinks all round. But a bloody replica? That would only ever lead to a never-ending nightmare. None of it adds up. That's why I believe, in spite of popular underworld opinion, that silly Gary probably did pull the replica gun on the coppers and go for the big bluff. You would have to have more bluff than brains to do it, but when you think you are in a corner you play the hand you have got and Gary tried to bluff a joker against a deck of aces, poor bugger.

I feel sorry for him, but why did he do it? Then again, if Lockwood and Avon did murder Gary and load him up with a replica then I am sure they will get theirs, as life gets everyone in the end.

I was once attacked by a crazy Greek wielding a plastic rubbish bin and I was holding a sawn-off shotgun. People flip out when they think they are in a corner. I think the boy just flipped out and went for whatever he could lay his hands on, and it proved a very fatal error of judgment. It's all a bit sad. Oh well, as the Chinese say, we live in interesting times. Except for Gary and his mate Jed Houghton, that is. In the end they found out that keeping bad company can give you lead poisoning.

CHAPTER 16

SCREWING SCREWS

ON March 7, 1993, two dangerous criminals, Peter Robert Gibb, a convicted killer and armed robber, and fellow killer Archie Butterly, escaped from the Melbourne Remand Centre with the aid of a prison officer, Heather Dianne Parker.

Parker, married with two children, was having an affair with Gibb, who persuaded her to smuggle explosives into the jail to help the pair escape. It is believed she had replica cell keys made to allow the men out. Gibb and Butterly then used the explosives to blast out an external wall and climbed down using knotted sheets.

The escapers drove off in a stolen car, but were followed by a prison officer in a taxi. The criminals crashed the getaway car, injuring Butterly, but they stole a motorbike and crashed again. When two police tried to arrest them, Butterly shot Senior Constable Warren Treloar in the chest and left arm.

The pair escaped and were later treated at the Moe hospital before they moved with Parker to the Gaffney's Creek Hotel, which they are believed to have set on fire next day. The historic 1865 brick hotel was burnt to the ground.

Six days after the escape police searching remote bushland near the head of the Goulburn River said they were fired upon by a machine gun. The Special Operations Group was called in and a 30-minute gun battle erupted.

Gibb and Parker were arrested as they tried to wade across the Goulburn River. Their accomplice, Butterly, was found dead with a bullet wound behind the right ear.

Police believe Butterly, who was badly injured from the car accident, might have been shot by Gibb. It is not known if Butterly asked to be shot rather than be recaptured.

Parker, who had previously been accused by other prison staff of having an affair with Gibb, was married to a prison officer. It was alleged she had been caught in a compromising position with Gibb in a jail cupboard.

'We all knew what was going on,' one prison officer said later. 'It was the worst kept secret in the jail.'

Parker was allegedly paid $25,000 by the popular entertainment television program '60 Minutes' to tell her story.

Police from the assets seizure unit began an investigation to see if any money paid by '60 Minutes' and 'Woman's Day' could be seized under laws prohibiting profit from crime.

Police raided the offices of 'Woman's Day' and the home of Parker's friend and publisher Andrea Hamilton-Vaughan, looking for evidence of payments.

In May, 1994, Parker, 30, was convicted in the Melbourne County Court of one count each of breaching a prison, rescuing a prisoner and causing serious injury.

She was also convicted of five counts of attempting to cause serious injury, four counts of each of theft, and using a firearm to prevent arrest, three counts of going equipped for theft, one of theft and making a threat to kill. In October the County Court ordered that Parker forfeit $42,000 under the Crimes (Confiscation of Profits) Act.

Gibb, then 39, was found guilty of rescuing a prisoner, causing serious injury and theft. He was also convicted of five counts of having attempted to cause serious injury, four counts each of armed robbery and using a firearm to prevent arrest and two counts of making a threat to kill. He had earlier pleaded guilty to escape.

During the trial Gibb and Parker would often whisper, touch or wink to each other. Friends said they were very much in love. Other prison officers claim Gibb would have killed Parker once he was free.

HOW do I love thee? Let me count the ways. I love thee the length and breadth of the Remand Centre. I love thee under the table, and on top of it as well.

I love thee in my cell when you pop in for that quick cell search. I love thee in every nook and cranny of the whole prison, providing no bugger is watching.

With any luck, 'my Princess in blue' I will love thee in the getaway car, providing you remember to leave the bloody doors unlocked.

I have liked a few warders in the past, but you, my little turnkey in suspenders, will always be my perfect screw . . .

Excuse the bad Shakespeare, but the story of Peter Gibb and his perfect screw touched my heart even in far-off Tasmania. It proved that true love is not dead. How could the romantics amongst us not be touched by such a love story?

Little Miss Parker joined the prison service to serve, and she didn't beat around the bush – or bush about the beat, in this case.

But don't be mistaken. Little Miss Parker, the bluestone babe who turned the key on Peter Gibb's heart, with one hand on the cell door and the other hand down his pants, is not the only lusty wench to have joined the ranks of the prison service. It always surprises many that there are so many spunky-looking ladies who work in the prison service and are prepared to serve any bloke, no matter whether he is a prison officer or prisoner.

Sex is not all that hard to get in Pentridge, if you know who to ask. I have heard of hard cash changing hands, in the case of one young lady who charged $100 for some extra stress relief. It was an outrageous asking price, but the inmates were in no position to argue, let alone argue the position.

There was no shortage of cash in Pentridge and the young female prison officer was swallowing the evidence every day she was on duty for about six months. Then she fell in love with one of her regular clients, and got caught by other prison officers humping his brains out.

She had to leave Pentridge in disgrace, but she was only one of many who got a bit too close to the job. Some of these officers have married former inmates.

Even as I write this, no doubt somewhere in Australia there is a female prison officer reading a love note that has been stuffed down her shirt by some hot-blooded inmate.

I have seen one glamorous gal in a blue uniform in the most compromising position with one of the nation's worst sex offenders, and she was loving it.

But it is not just female prison officers and the inmates involved. I have known the male staff to be involved with their female counterparts.

Nightshift with the right female staff member can be party time for the rest of the staff. One lady was caught doing the job under the desk. Perhaps they were just playing nude Twister.

And there have been female members of staff caught in each other's arms.

The sex stories in the big slammer are never ending.

Females too dizzy to get into the police force seem to be welcome in Pentridge, and while there are some solid, hard-working, honest and straight women who work in jails, there are others who just cause trouble. I would say that 80 per cent of them are solid as rocks but the other 20 per cent run riot in a sexual sense. They create trouble because jealousy leads to violence. They play one prisoner against another, one screw against another. It only takes one trollop to screw her way through inmates and prison officers in one division to cause a riot within a month.

I could name seven female prison staff who have been involved in everything from heroin trafficking to selling sexual favors.

It is the sex that causes the trouble. All female prison officers should be horse whipped at the gate, not only in the name of security, but for the common good. I have never seen the sense of allowing females to work in a male prison. In the first place, they are first, last and always, a security risk, and a total waste of space.

The smell of perfume in the air in a men's prison can be very hard to take, let me tell you. It would be kinder to prisoners to kick female staff out and to hell with the Equal Opportunity Commission. Common sense should prevail.

So what's the attraction? Why *do* women want to work in a male prison?

Don't ask me to explain some of the unlikely love stories that have happened behind bars, because love is a mystery none of us can explain.

Personally, I have never screwed a screw. I am somewhat of a criminal snob, after all. It is my long held view that one does not hump prison officers or police, no matter how beautiful they may be, and no matter how tempting the offer. It's a form of fraternising which can only lead to unhappiness, in my view.

One female screw blew up a condom in front of me, tied a knot in it and then signed her name on it with a texta color. She thought it was a joke, but to me it was teasing of the worst kind. Another would spray perfume on your pillow and kiss the pillow with a mouthful of lipstick. That sort of stuff does no-one any good.

It might be funny for them, and it might give some of the bent bitches a thrill, but those capers can send you silly when you're locked up all the time. No, I say they should get women officers out of prison before they get some poor bugger killed. It will happen. It could be an inmate, or it could be a member of staff. Some of these ladies are downright dangerous.

Little Miss Heather Parker is tame compared to some of the dirty girls in blue.

I've known Peter Gibb for 20 years. He is an old hood who grew up in Prahran. The first time he came to my attention was at a dance in Prahran, when a handgun dropped out of his pants and hit the floor. All eyes turned to see a somewhat embarrassed and sheepish Peter bend down to pick up the offending firearm and try to tip-toe out without drawing attention to himself.

He was always good at pulling the girls and little Miss Parker, if my memory serves me correctly, would be the third female prison officer to fall for Peter's glib tongue.

They all gave Peter their hearts, as well as their panties.

He must have a good line of conversation because I have seen Peter in the showers, and believe me, he hasn't got a big line in anything else. Ha ha.

But some of these blokes could talk the pants off the Pope's mother and I suspect Peter Gibb is one of them.

While I applaud true love, and it is nice to see romance raise its head, in this hard, cold world such goings on can be fatal.

In little Miss Parker's case, true love found a way, but it got poor Archie Butterly blown away.

As I've just said, jails are no place for women because they drive men mad, but it does have its moments. One day here in Risdon my little mate Bucky pulled out his old fella on a female prison officer known around the jail as the 'chewing gum blonde'. Bucky yelled out to her: 'Hey, Pudden, get over here and get a bit of this into ya'.

The chewing gum blonde, who always has a mouth full of gum, looked at Bucky, then down at the offending member and yelled back: 'Put it away, you little idiot. I've seen better bits of meat hanging off the butcher's pencil.' Which wasn't a bad comeback, but it didn't worry Bucky. 'Yeah,' he said, 'well get over here and drop your drawers and I'll knock a string of farts out of you that ya wouldn't believe.'

That's what I think poor old Peter Gibb should have done to Heather Parker ... knocked a string of farts out of her, and left it at that. What a bloody mess. And poor old Archie Butterly spent his last six days on earth out in the bush listening to Peter Gibb hump the guts out of little Miss Parker. Bloody hell, if I was out the bush with those two and I'd be saying: 'Come on, Pete. Whack up.'

Someone shot poor Archie. I wonder who?

One doesn't like to make light of true love, but this time around I can't help it. I remember little Miss (or I should say Mrs) Parker from when she worked at Pentridge, and I recall her as a stuck-up little miss with a bad attitude.

I dead set hate female screws. What the hell are these cows doing in a man's prison? They do nothing but create trouble, jealousy, frustration and anger. Who wants to look at these molls prancing about the jail trying to look tough?

Peter Gibb is a harmless enough poor bugger in spite of a dangerous reputation, and I've got nothing against him personally, but bloody female screws are lower than shark shit in my opinion, and a very dangerous thing to have in an all-male prison. The bloody things should be driven out the front gate with horse whips. I spit on them all.

CHAPTER 17

THE PASSING OF H DIVISION

IN August 1994 the Victorian Government finally closed the most notorious section of the prison system, H Division. It was the high security division where inmates broke rocks as punishment, and where Ronald Ryan, the last man hanged in Australia, spent his last few hours before his execution in 1967.

Of the infamous criminals who spent time in the 37-cell division, prison officers remember one above them all – Chopper Read.

THE end of H Division is the end of a part of my life. It might sound totally insane, but H Division was my own personal kingdom. I was the general of an army of psychopaths that no horror movie could ever do justice.

It was the place where we made our own rules. I used all my tactical and strategic expertise. My rule was total and without question. I put together a crew of nutters never before seen in any prison, and we waged a prison war which went on for years.

It was the sort of violence that only ever existed in war. God, I loved it. It is the gang war which is now part of Victorian jail legend.

142

It wasn't the only gang war that I was involved in. I took part in many, and through cunning, strength and good luck, I survived them all. But as far as tactics were concerned, the H Division fracas was the classic. It was text book physical combat and psychological warfare. It was there that I learnt that a small army of blood loyal deranged allies could defeat an army of established criminal families. They had the names, the networks, the backup and the reputations. We had the courage, the ruthlessness and the tactics.

Keithy Faure and the dockies were tough, there is no doubt about that, but the Overcoat gang, led by my good self, was tougher. I had been taught by my old Dad, Vincent Villeroy and Billy 'The Texan' Longley, and I used these tactics to the full.

I turned H Division into my own personal fortress. The end of H is the end of a large part of my past life. I know it sounds insane, but I loved that division. That is why I would win the battles. The other inmates hated the place and suffered because of it. I loved it and it was never too hard for me.

The modern prison is a marshmallow compared with good old H. It was the last place from the old hard school and in my heart I preferred the old days to the system that we have now. A good flogging can concentrate the mind.

I did 10½ years in 'H,' the so-called blood house of the system. It wasn't just my home, I owned the place.

I owned it, I controlled it, I ran it. By ruling that division we ran the jail. We were the most feared gang in the most feared division of the most feared jail in Australia, and I was the commanding general.

I ran a five-year gang war from within the walls of H Division. And we had the power and influence to reach out from behind those walls.

The power we had was never really understood or appreciated except by our enemies, who understood very well indeed. H Division scarred the bodies and minds of generations of so-called hard men. Even the prison staff were scarred, not to mention scared.

Why is it that every time I wave at a psychiatrist from a distance of 300 metres he tosses a handful of pills down my neck? I have been put on Xanax and mentally speaking, I feel like I'm being held in the Whitbury Newtown Leisure Centre. They have just given me my nightly 'bomb me out pill' and the white clouds are rolling in.

Any rate, enough of this. My double dose of Mogadon is just beginning to kick in. My grandfather was as mad as a hatter, my father has just got out from the psychiatric ward of the Launceston Hospital. I'm now left to wonder what nut house I'll end up in. Ah, mental insanity, the last refuge of the true genius. Ha ha. Goodnight.

I have decided to tell the shrinks to jam the medication up their anally retentive bottoms, and I am going to face life with a clear mind. I have seen that many psychiatrists I am quite confident that I could put up my sanity against theirs and still get some change. It is not a profession that gives you confidence in the stability of its occupants.

I have pulled all the pictures of girls from my walls. I have become sick and tired of prison staff and other inmates perving on pictures of some of my good friends who happen to be female.

There have been many rude comments made about an old friend of mine, Melissa Bentley. Every sex maniac and rapist in jail would call in for a daily perve. There were about 70 photos, many of them of fans of the books who were kind enough to send their pictures to me.

But I have decided to get rid of them because with some of the comments made about them I would end up pulling some bastard's eye out, which would not look good when I am trying to convince the High Court that I am the male version of Mother Teresa. So I have put up pictures of the Derwent Valley in their place. It has helped calm everyone down, me included. I have never had a dream of covering the Derwent Valley with whipped cream and then licking it off.

The last one off the wall was a poster of Samantha Fox. I kissed her goodbye and gave her to a young bloke doing six years for rape. I'm sure she wouldn't mind.

Michael Hodgman, QC, MP, always insists that I polish up before we have a court date. As I've mentioned I have been forced to wear a Liberal Party tie so that I look smart enough to attend court.

Michael is a Hutchins private school old boy which is part of the Tassie establishment.

He was representing some old ratbag scallywag who was dressed like a St Vincent de Paul reject and was the town drunk. Mick wanted him to look spick and span before he went to court before an old stick- in-the-mud judge who is no longer with us.

Mr Hodgman, the kind-hearted soul he is, lent his client a clean shirt and a tie, which as luck would have it, was the respected Hutchins school tie.

The judge looked horrified to see this bloke, who looked like a dog's dinner, sitting before him in the dock. It became clear very early that this bloke was as guilty as sin. The judge must have felt sympathetic because he said: 'Guilty, but I don't think we need bother your client with a jail sentence.'

The shocked client walked free. Perish the thought that the old school tie did the trick.

THE MOUTH FROM THE SOUTH

From Queenstown to Hobart Town,
From Canberra to Darling Downs,
He's fought a thousand battles,
In a hundred different towns,
And while he's very sober,
And always in good condition,
He's a soap box battler,
A dinkum Aussie politician,
And while most just call him Michael,

When they're drunk they call him Mick,
They know the Mouth from the South,
Will never miss a trick.
The champion of the underdog,
And the drinking man's friend,
He'll start a fight then finish it,
And take it to the end,
And when it comes to trouble, boy,
He don't ever run and hide,
And when your back's against the wall,
You'll find him at your side,
And when the Devil comes a knocking,
He'll stick there to the end,
And I'm proud I even shook his hand,
He's the Aussie battler's friend.

CHAPTER 18

CHRISTOPHER DALE FLANNERY

FOR well over 12 months I have had a chap named Ian Hill ringing and wanting to come and see me about the death of Christopher Dale Flannery, the idiot they called Mr Rent-A-Kill who went on the missing list in Sydney in May, 1985.

In a previous book I said that I had been told that he had been killed and his body put through a tree shredder in country Victoria.

Mr Hill is working on the inquest into Flannery's death. There has been more work put into the death of this no-account hood and contract killer than into the death of Harold Holt.

It is typical of Sydney gangster-obsessed bullshit that so much time and effort be spent on so little. We know what happened to Chris – he got offed and a good thing, too.

Everyone with a barrow to push has jumped on board the Flannery hearse. Brain dead crims are jumping up and trying to give evidence. Many of them are looking for the cushy life in witness protection or so they can get their ugly heads on telly.

There have been sightings of Flannery having dinner with Elvis

Presley. My only knowledge of Flannery was passed on to me by two
good crooks who are now both dead. I have no intention of joining
the circus in Sydney about the death of a contract killer. I didn't like
the nitwit when he was alive and I have no intention of carrying on
about him now that he is dead.

Anyrate, I really know what happened to Harry Holt. He couldn't
swim too well. Ha ha.

THE Flannery business became totally bloody ludicrous when I was
served (on September 9, 1994) with a rather unique form of
summons to appear as a witness at the inquest into his death ... at 10
o'clock in the forenoon at Risdon Prison, if you don't mind.

This application was made by the same Ian David Hill, solicitor
for the State Coroner. It would appear quite unique in that 'the
mountain is coming to Muhammad'. That is, the buggers weren't too
keen on the idea of moving me to NSW, so they've got themselves a
nice little trip to Tassie.

I see myself entering into the world of high farce, although the
legal chaps in NSW in charge of the whole Flannery debacle take it
all very seriously, in keeping with their NSW gangster fixation.

While this might not be a first in legal history, it's certainly the first
summons of this type I've heard of. Hence my use of the word
'ludicrous'. After this business I never again want to hear the word
'Flannery'.

The inquest hearing was held on September 13. And God, what a
day it was. I spent half of it being questioned by a Mr Peter Johnston,
the senior counsel investigating the Flannery debacle, with junior
counsel Mr Rick Hensley faithfully assisting the rather serious Mr
Johnston, and Mr Ian Hill standing by operating the tape recording
equipment.

All was well until they dug out a photostat copy of a very old
personal address book cum diary that I'd kept along with others
from 1970 to 1987, and the ghosts from Christmases past all came

back to haunt me. A lot of the names in it belonged to people who are now dead. Some of them were would-be targets and people to keep an eye on, and there were general comic remarks and odd thoughts.

The names, addresses, and phone numbers of every one from Abe Saffron to Andrew Peacock were in that book. A lot of them I didn't know, but for one reason or another, way back when, I had occasion to jot down personal details of police, crooks, bookies, mice and millionaires. A sort of toecutter's memory notebook. In the hands of suspicious and paranoid investigators it must have looked quite odd: phone numbers and addresses and personal details of old gang leaders and drug dealers, old girl friends and Masonic Lodge contacts, Italians and police, politicians and poofters and blue-eyed pussy cats ... the whole rambling lot of flapdoodle that a young psycho toecutter might wish to jot down and hold onto for a rainy day.

There was gossip I'd heard, names of the dead and who I thought might have done it, contracts put to me re this one and that one and not taken up, phone numbers of girls I knew from when I was 15 to 30. But even though I knew it was harmless there were remarks re Flannery and friends and contacts of the dear departed, and phone numbers and addresses relating to them, and names of Mr Bigs and Mr Not So Bigs from various ethnic backgrounds, overseas phone numbers and names and numbers in code. It was a blast from my highly insane past, and some of it must have looked suspicious.

The notebook was one of four that I kept. The other three I know have been destroyed. However, I'd not only forgotten all about the fourth but I also remember wondering to myself whatever happened to that fourth book. It makes me not guilty of anything – just sort of guilty of everything. And, naturally, it seemed of great interest to the gentlemen investigating the Flannery fiasco.

Johnston, Hensley and Hill were all very correct and businesslike and serious, in between trying to maintain a straight face at my tone of conversation. Rick Hensley let the side down now and again with a display of silent laughter. Johnston and Hill did their best to maintain that cold, professional, no-nonsense stiff upper lip, although I did detect a touch of amusement in them, despite their best efforts to repress it.

I really hope I've heard the last of Flannery, Harold Holt and Azaria Chamberlain ... can we please just wave them all goodbye?

A SHORT postscript relating to my meeting with the legal team from NSW of Johnston, Hensley and Hill – a small point of common courtesy and old fashioned good manners.

It was not the first inquest into someone's death at which I've had to appear. And, over the years, I've been introduced to some very senior counsel and some very senior police in Victoria and Tasmania, and without exception each and every one has politely introduced themselves with the extended hand. In other words, when men meet in Aussie land, hands are shaken. I've shaken hands with politicians, judges, high-ranking prosecutors and top policemen. It is a common Aussie form of polite, old-fashioned basic courtesy and civil good manners.

However, when being introduced to the legal team of Johnston, Hensley and Hill no such common, decent courtesy was extended to me. It was a cool, businesslike case of 'thankyou Mr Read ... please sit down'. And when it was over, it was just 'thankyou and goodbye', with no handshake.

In my opinion, this is the height of bad manners, discourtesy, and downright rudeness, and is typical of the la de da 'we come from NSW' snob attitude.

After all, I'm just Chopper Read the crook. But I'm one crook who has shaken hands with more heavyweights in all walks of life than most uppity NSW lawyers will get to meet in a lifetime. I hate discourtesy.

CHAPTER 19

THE ONES THAT GOT AWAY... THANK GOD

THE news in July that my old Dad had been taken to hospital with a suspected cancer gave me a shock that brought back floods of sentimental memories. Dad has been in many ways my saving grace, the voice of reason injecting a note of common sense into situations I was involved in, resulting in lives being saved instead of taken.

Some of these situations are so far-fetched that if I told a donkey he would kick me in the head for telling lies.

Such as the plot to kill probably the most famous Australian Catholic of the past 50 years, Mr Bob Santamaria, the leader of the National Civic Council.

It all went back to the fact that my dad was a master mason in the Masonic Lodge and also a member of the Orange Lodge. Well, he was until he and about 3000 other masons baled out of the lodge in the late 1960s and early 1970s because of internal upheaval in the fraternity.

For a short time many years ago I myself was affiliated with a renegade group of outlawed freemasons known as the Black Chapter

Masons or Orange Masons – the 'Brethren of the Black Chapter Antient Charge 6.4, sublime sons of Hiram Abriff'.

My old comrade in arms Vincent Villeroy was a member of the same outlawed order. I won't go into the political details of the Black Chapter, but they were against the mainstream Freemasons, namely the Blue Lodge Masons, allowing Catholics to enter their ranks. All of this is a bit meaningless now, because the craft or masonic lodge of today is a piss poor shadow of what it once stood for.

But in 1974 it was still big deal. It was that year old Roy H., Vincent Villeroy and a handful of other brothers of the Black Chapter let me in on a mad cap plot to kill B.A. Santamaria. This plot to kill took place in the bar of the Tower Hotel in Collingwood and involved some dozen or more crazy old Orange drum bangers who'd left the Freemasons. Cash was raised and a plan was put together with the idea that Santamaria's murder would be blamed on members of the Australian Communist Party. Ha ha.

And it would have happened – except that my old Dad put the knocker on it with a passionate verbal tirade about political assassination being un-Australian, and forbidding me from having any role in it. My withdrawal meant that Vincent Villeroy baled out, followed by old Roy, and the whole insane plot died a natural death because we were the only ones with the guts and guns to do the job.

While men like Bob Santamaria are remembered by history, men like my Dad are forgotten. Yet Santamaria owes his life to my old Dad.

And if anybody doubts this, it reminds me of another yarn which might pull them up and make them think.

HAVE you ever noticed how old tunes get caught in your head and sort of become your favorite song. Mine has always been Frankie Lane singing *High Noon* ... 'Do not forsake me darlin' on this our wedding day'.

Dave the Jew would often sing a sad old song. I don't know the name of it, but it went 'And the chapel bells were ringing in the little country town, and the little congregation prayed for little Jimmy Brown'.

Old Bruno C., who we called 'Poppa', would burst into song with *Ave Maria,* like some out of tune Placido Domingo. Bruno was a good old Sicilian pirate, and Dave the Jew was a bonny buccaneer, but like myself neither of them could hold a note. Vincent Villeroy, on the other hand, had a beautiful singing voice, with his strong Northern Irish accent.

Anyway, one night Dave the Jew, Poppa, Vincent Villeroy and myself were parked in Vincent's old Pontiac in the street, and old Poppa said to Vincent: 'Hey, Vinnie, sing us a song. You gotta da beautiful a voice'. So Vinnie started singing his favorite song and – this is no joke – it was *Thank You For Just Being You* by Lionel Rose, the former world bantamweight champion. It was a God-awful song, but when Vincent sang it, it would bring a tear to a glass eye. But when he finished, the Jew passed a sarcastic remark that any man who held Lionel Rose up as a great singing talent had his taste buds in his arse, and was not guilty of heavyweight musical appreciation.

Vincent turned around and said 'what would you know about musical appreciation, ya little kike nutcase?'

Dave pulled out his trusty Scott Webley .38 calibre revolver and pointed it at Vincent's head, and Vincent said: 'Ahh, go on and pull the trigger, ya crazy little kike nutter'.

'No-one calls me a kike!' yells Dave. Vincent just starts to sing *Thank You For Just Being You* and Dave starts up with 'And the chapel bells were ringing in the little country town, and the little congregation prayed for little Jimmy Brown'.

Poppa and me got out of the car, and left Dave holding a pistol at Vincent's head and both of them singing different songs at the top of their voices at 1am.

As Poppa and I walked along the road trying to hail a taxi, he said to me: 'Chopper, that Jew boy he a gonna kill us all a one a day, or get us all a killed – and he can't bloody sing either'. Ha ha.

And you know where we were parked that night?

Across the road from 1207 Burke Road in Kew. Bob Santamaria's house.

THE biggest thing I miss in jail – apart from sex, guns, and Irish whiskey – is gambling. Roulette in particular. But in my sentimental day dreams I always return to the racetrack, where the rich and famous mix freely with the vulgar multitude. Gee, I've had some laughs on race tracks. I got to see some of the greatest horses in racing history run, and I've got to meet some of racing's legends, like Mr R.W. Trinder, the owner of Piping Lane, the winner of the 1972 Melbourne Cup. And Old Tommy Woodcock, Phar Lap's strapper – and trainer for a short time before the Yanks killed the great horse in New Mexico. Old Tommy was a wonderful old bloke but prone to tears whenever the name of the great Phar Lap was mentioned. And on meeting Tommy how could you avoid asking some small question in relation to the greatest horse who ever ran a race?

I shook hands with Sir Henry Bolte at the 1971 Caulfield Cup after Mick Mallyon had just ridden Gay Icarus to victory. On a race track, when everyone is full of piss and good will, everyone seems to be everyone's mate. Especially since I was in the company of one of the most feared old 'gunnies' in Melbourne, Horatio Morris.

I stood in the betting ring at the 1974 Melbourne Cup with Vincent Villeroy and Dave the Jew and I told this la de da old toff to whack all his dough on Leilani on the nose. Leilani had just won the Caulfield Cup. The old toff took my advice. He introduced himself as Henry. He turned out to be Sir Henry Winneke, the Governor of Victoria. I mean, you meet every bugger at the race track. Incidentally, he did his dough. She ran second.

Seeing as I've mentioned Leilani winning the Caulfield Cup, I will tell a little tale about her owner, the Liberal politician Andrew Peacock, and his then wife.

We were all a bit pissed off – me and the Jew, Vincent Villeroy and our crew – as we had put a packet on Turfcutter to win, and the bloody thing came in third. Anyway, over a few drinks, we thought it would be a good idea to pinch the Caulfield Cup. Ha ha.

Evidently, Andrew Peacock's wife Susan was running rampant throughout every fashionable nightclub in Toorak and South Yarra dancing on table tops and drinking champagne out of the Caulfield Cup – a habit she got quite a name for later when her next husband's horse Beldale Ball won the Melbourne Cup in 1980.

Anyway, me and the Jew and Vincent drove to Monomeath Avenue, Canterbury – number 30 to be exact – where Peacock was living at that time, and waited at a discreet distance for Susan to return home. We got sick of waiting by about 3am, so then we waited outside a fashionable restaurant in Toorak Road, South Yarra. Again we missed out. By this time we had sobered up. We had no intention of harming Susan. We were just going to do a friendly snatch and grab on the Caulfield Cup.

Oh well. Just one more two-bob, nitwit plan down the drain. But I must admit I've had some great times on racetracks. They are the best places on earth, next to brothels and casinos. I suspect it will be some time before I see another Caulfield Cup, more's the pity.

MY mind keeps turning to the 1970s. At my very first Melbourne Cup Dave the Jew won $1500 on Baghdad Note, after I had lost my life savings of $1100 at the Caulfield Cup the week before, when Dave had won $1200 on Beer Street. He had uncanny luck for a so-called non-punter.

I remember Horatio Morris introduced me, Dave the Jew, and Cowboy Johnny Harris to the great Sammy Lee of Les Girls fame. He owned the Ritz Hotel in St Kilda and owned nightclubs all over Sydney, and was a one-time partner of that well-known Sydney nightclub owner and gambling identity Mr Perce Galea.

As it happened, Sammy Lee, a flashily-dressed, loud-mouthed, Yankee-accented, pimpy looking ponce, spoke Yiddish and chatted away to Dave the Jew like a long-lost brother. Very few people ever knew that Sammy Lee, the man who built a nightclub empire, was a Jew boy whose real name was Samuel Levi. It is a small world, because Vincent Villeroy and the late Joe Borg – Vincent was Borg's bodyguard – had once bashed Sammy Lee near to death outside the Latin Quarter night club in Pitt Street, Sydney, in 1967.

Joe Borg, the vice king of Sydney, got blown to bits in a car bombing the following year, 1968, and Vincent fled to Melbourne, never to return to NSW. But again I digress, as I have a bad habit of doing.

I met Sammy Lee at the 1971 Melbourne Cup, the one Silver Knight won, and Sammy Lee invited us all to the Ritz Hotel for a party. It was a mistake for Sammy, as it turned out, but my crew had a great time.

Dave the Jew nearly killed a female impersonator after he discovered 'she' was a he. Then Cowboy Johnny gave Sammy Lee's bodyguard, a middleweight boxer called Angelo, a left hook that broke his jaw. All in drunken jest, of course. To top it off, Vincent walked in with a very drunk Micky Tollis, and when poor Sammy Lee saw Vincent he nearly had a heart attack and fled to the showgirls' dressing room and locked himself in. His bodyguard Angelo had already taken a taxi to the Alfred Hospital to get his busted jaw wired up.

Ahh, the 1970s, they do indeed evoke sentimental memories. Poor old Sammy Lee with his black shirt, black pants, white sports coat and white slip-on shoes. He died in 1975, poor old la de da Yankee faggot. He wasn't really a bad bloke, the Jew boy who told everyone he was a Russian.

All this brings me to another story that could have ended up with a lime funeral, but didn't.

It happened one day at Moonee Valley. Me, Dave the Jew and Vincent Villeroy stood and watched 'Eddie the Fireman' Birchley stick 50 thousand bucks on one horse – and win. (This was 1973, the same year Gala Supreme won the Melbourne Cup.) Dave the Jew wanted to kill Eddie Birchley, but me and Vincent wouldn't allow it. Call us sentimental fools, if you like, but 'The Fireman' was part of racing history. I mean, you had to have some respect. It was a privilege just to watch him in action. His ilk are all gone now.

GIVING up smoking when Dad got sick this year has affected me. The lack of nicotine in my system has sent my mind into outer space and my memory is getting sharper. I seem to have that old edge all over again – a sort of inner rage welling up in me – and I'm recalling old memories from long ago. The art of not letting the inner rage show and maintaining the smiling mask escapes me once in a while, but I try hard.

Many years ago Dave the Jew, Vincent Villeroy and my old Sicilian mate Poppa, now dead, got together with myself to discuss two topics ... namely Nappy Ollington, the two-up king of Melbourne, and 'Tuppence' Moran, who was allegedly mixed up in a big SP bookie ring.

Old Poppa felt that we could all 'make-a-da bigga money if we gotta ridda these two pricks'. His idea of English was a sorta like-a that. Ha ha. God bless him.

Back then Nappy Ollington was very friendly with Charlie Wooton, Putty Nose Nicholls, Dougie Sproule, the late Pat Shannon, old Pat Cartwright, 'Machinegun' Bobby Dix, Brian and Les Kane and young up and comers in the form of 'Young Al' and another bloke called Mick. Back then, Al and Mick hung around the two-up and sort of acted as bouncers.

Nearly the whole ruling body of the Victorian Federated Ship Painters and Dockers were friends of Nappy Ollington – including Jackie Twist, Joey Turner and the rest. And then you had a list of police and politicians a mile long. And bloody Tuppence Moran had almost as many connections as Nappy.

But there were two men that Nappy and Tuppence didn't have on side, and they were Billy 'The Texan' Longley, and old Poppa. So, as far as I was concerned, to hell with Ollington and Moran. 'Piss on them both' was Dave the Jew's attitude. In one fell swoop we could make a lot of money and do both Longley and Poppa a kindness.

However, again it wasn't to be. A high-ranking policeman got to hear of things, and intervened. And because this policeman was a friend of my father's and a leading Freemason I walked away, and the Jew and Vincent followed me.

I was polite, and I smiled, and I was courteous, and so I agreed to leave it alone. But the rage within me boiled. Life is made up of compromise, give and take, doing a favor to get a favor, and walking away when you want to attack.

And Nappy Ollington and Tuppence Moran are luckier gamblers than they ever knew.

CHAPTER 20

A CELL WITH A VIEW

AS I sit in my cell writing this on a bitter cold Sunday morning my hands are a mixture of dead numb and pins and needles. It is so cold in my cell you could hang meat in it, but it is warmer in the cell than outside.

It is quite beautiful when I come out of the cell in the morning. It is dark dawn and the cloud, or fog, hangs heavy just above the roof cage of the prison yard, and as I look at the hills that surround the prison it is as if the clouds or fog have cut them in half.

It is a very surreal, yet quite beautiful sight. I will never grow tired of casting my eyes toward the tree-covered hills around this place. It is a lovely view and the hills look so close that I could reach out and touch them. I can even see the fire tracks and walking paths that wind their way through between the trees.

If someone walked up these hills and stood and waved we could see them quite clearly and wave back. Every night or afternoon as I walk back with the rest of B yard, from our mess room to our cells for the night, I cast my eyes over these tree-covered hills. It is a wonderful sight for a bloke in prison.

The trouble is most of the guys here have come from the logging industry. They look at the trees and you can nearly hear the chainsaws start up in their heads.

In Pentridge the best view available to me on a good day was the bloody Kodak factory, about a mile away across some paddocks.

This jail has an almost make believe feel to it. It is a Clayton's prison – the jail you're in when you're not really in jail. Or a pixie prison from a tall tales nursery rhyme. I wake up every morning with the feeling that none of it is real.

It is a very petty, silly little place, yet very cosy and comfy and relaxed, like the sort of jail you'd send your old granny to. The fact that they take themselves so seriously is all part of its totally ridiculous comic magic.

I feel as if I'm the prisoner of a Monty Python joke in a Dennis Potter movie, especially once a week when the farmer's daughter comes in to visit me. The thought of Chopper and the posh farmer's daughter has created some scallywag comedy around the prison.

One of the prison staff joked with me the other day, 'Hey Chopper, how much do you love this girl' and Bucky yelled out from behind me '30 grand an acre, that's how much.'

Everyone laughed, but it was a bit hurtful, even though I found myself joining in the comedy of it all. What am I going to do with Mary-Ann when I get out of this place – if I ever get out? I don't want to lose her, but I don't want to cause her unhappiness either.

When you're in jail and a woman starts to visit you she has a captive audience and the poor bugger behind bars comes to depend on her visits and a love develops, and when the prisoner gets out of jail he feels a deep obligation to repay this debt of love and loyalty.

It's a case of 'I stuck with you when you were in jail, now you make my dream come true'. It is like befriending a wounded wild animal in a cage and over a period of time the animal teaches himself or learns to trust you, rely on you, count on you, depend on you, and love you. Then one day the cage is gone and the animal is free.

This is what happened with me and Margaret. I went from a prison of bluestone walls and iron bars into a prison of mental and emotional guilt, caused by a deep sense of obligation to repay love and loyalty. I used to stand on the back steps of our place in Launceston, which was full of thousands of dollars worth of domestic household bullshit that women love so much and I'd say 'Margaret, I love you, but I'm telling you right now I'm not happy inside my own heart'.

I don't want to be mentally and emotionally kidnapped while I'm in jail and walk free of one prison only to be taken into another of pots and pans, washing machines, fridges and freezers, microwave ovens, double beds and doonas, lounge suites and new carpets, drapes and knick knacks on the wall, with some nagging female giving me hell for not coming home on time for my din dins, and wanting to grab her bloody handbag and come with me every time I head for the door.

'Where are you going? Where have you been? What are you doing? What have you done?' This is the nightmare women put you in.

You don't want to lose them but you don't want to become their bloomin' prisoner either. Bucky asked me what would I do if I got out and was on my own? My answer was that if I had my own way I'd get out and live in my mate's pub, write books to pay the bills, bang the tail off every dirty girl I could get my hands on, gamble my guts out and drink myself to death. I mean, really, is that too much to ask?

And if things don't work out with me and Mary-Ann when I get out of this shit, that's exactly what I will do. Just live in a pub by the sea, write books and be on my own. Maybe Damian Bugg QC could come over for a holiday.

Mind you, Mary-Ann is clever. She knows all this and tells me she won't let it happen. Time will tell. It seems that not only is the jail I'm in surreal, but my whole life is becoming more and more dreamlike. And the more that life crashes in on me the more that room in a pub by the sea sounds good to me. Write a couple more books before I die, pouring Irish whiskey down my neck as I go, spinning out on the roulette wheel and pulling on a few hot little blondes along the way before I climb quietly into my coffin.

Bugger what you think, it sounds great to me.

BY May down here it's winter as far as I am concerned. Mary-Ann sent me in some special 'Made in New Zealand' long underwear that they wear down at the South Pole and I sleep in the bloody things under seven blankets. I'm writing this with my overcoat on and with one glove on my left hand, and the hand I'm using to write with is nearly frozen.

It gets below freezing level in these cells at night. They have an electric heater bolted into the wall of every cell and we get three hours of heating per night which really means that the heater comes on in four and five minute bursts over a three-hour period and one five minute burst at about 5.30 in the morning.

Thank God the laundry where I work is warm. Eddy the head, the boss of the laundry, put me in charge of this big industrial size ironing machine and I feed damp pillow cases into it all day long with three blokes at the other end folding the bloody things up. The old ironing machine punches out some heat.

They put all the ratbags down the laundry and it's meant to be the worst job in the place, but I love it. In winter it's the only place to be. It even has its own showers.

When I got here there was talk of making me the new jail barber. But the Governor knocked that idea on the head so instead they gave the job to Micky bloody Chatters.

Micky is a top bloke and my friend, but he is the last bloke any sane person would want to see placed in charge of scissors. Let me tell you, if Micky walked into a shearing shed, the sheep would go on strike.

If a bloke came into Risdon charged with poisoning 100 people they would put him in charge of the kitchen.

CHOPPER 4

I'm still getting into trouble over the contents of my mail. They had a go at me last week for making mention of staff members by name in my letters. To call the Governor or any of the various deputies or staff members by name is forbidden, which means that when I write to Mary-Ann I am unable to use the name of her own sister, since Mary-Ann's sister took a job here as an education officer and actually sits on the bloody classification committee. Imagine me marrying into the classo board. God help us all!

Half the staff seems to be related, half the inmates seem to be related and a good quarter of both sides seem to be related to each other ... and I will probably be called up to the Governor's office for writing this. I've never encountered a situation like it before.

I've been in this jail about two years so far, and I haven't put a foot wrong. I haven't said a word out of place to a single soul. I am in reality a model prisoner, yet I am still looked upon as some sort of freak and viewed with suspicion and paranoia.

I'm so polite to the buggers it's almost sickening, and the more I smile the less they trust me and when I frown they trust me even less. Oh well, they can pay full price for the new book when it comes out.

As I write this the wind has turned funny and the night rain is blowing against my cell window and door. It's a strange sort of night. I know I've mentioned the word 'surreal' before but it really is. All I'm waiting for is for the Governor and a dozen or so of the prison staff to break out in song and dance and the Dennis Potter movie would be complete.

As I stand in the prison laundry all day long feeding damp pillow cases into the hot rollers of the ironing machine, I find myself spinning out into daydream land, or returning to the mental and emotional safety of the sentimental memories of my past. It's like *The Singing Detective*.

At night time in my sleep I escape the prison walls into the world of my dreams and during the daylight hours my mind dances or flutters between the cold reality of my situation and the surreal non-

168

reality of my day dreams. I travel back in my mind's eye to my childhood and teenage years.

Now that I'm nearing my 40th year my day dreams never sweep me away to the fantasy of the future, but to the best and sweetest times of my past. And despite the horrors of my past life, there have been some sweet and wonderful moments.

My mind is caught up in reliving a past adventure or a sentimental memory, but in jail it is like a fantasy. Was I really there? Did I really do that? Was that person real? The past is like a fantasy as it is only a dream in your mind. The future is also only a dream. The only thing that is real is now, and now is always so boring, or so it seems.

Instead, we wonder what tomorrow will bring and while we await that adventure we recall with sentimental longing the magic of yesterday. The present, then, is only a boring waiting room between yesterday and tomorrow. For me, in jail, tomorrow brings nothing and so I look back to yesterday.

Memories ... of my father cracking his hard boiled eggs on my head as we sat together on the back steps. Memories of myself and the rest of the little school kids marching around the playground to the tune of Click *Go The Shears* at Thomastown State School. Memories of myself as a nine-year-old boy and the local gang of kids chipping in with all our pennies and halfpennies to come up with the princely sum of one shilling in order to bribe the mentally retarded girl who lived down the road to undo her shirt and show us her big tits.

We would stand there in true boyish wonder at the sight of it, or them, reaching up to feel if they were real.

Then afterwards we would con the poor girl with the big tits into buying a shilling's worth of hot chips with salt and vinegar for us all. In the early 60s a shilling's worth of chips would feed a small army.

As I stand there feeding the damp pillow cases into the hot rollers of the ironing machine my mind springs out into the memories of past insanities and magic adventures. Past sexual adventures that I thought little of at the time, yet have haunted my mind ever since my return to jail to drive me just that touch more insane than I already am.

Some women, once met, cast a spell on you and the memory of them haunts you till the grave, and I've met many such women in my time. Yes, my body is in prison but my mind is sailing in the wind. Thank God.

WHEN the breakfast, lunch or tea bell rings, we all stand on parade, and after our names are called out we have a ten-minute wait in line before we march off in a disorderly fashion to get our food.

It is on the muster line that some of the best comic remarks and conversations are to be had and heard. Although silence is meant to be maintained, it rarely, if ever, is.

It was there that I learned, to my horror, that the only two people on the whole muster who had ever heard of or seen the great movie classic *Cool Hand Luke,* starring Paul Newman, was myself and a Melbourne crook called Harry the Greek.

Paul Newman played the role of Lucas Jackson in the movie, which has influenced a generation of scallywags, crooks, knockabouts and tearaways.

It is an all-time classic and tells you about jail life. When Luke Jackson's mother dies he comes back into the chain gang barracks, picks up his old banjo and with tears in his eyes sings this song: 'I don't care if it rains or freezes, long as I've got my plastic Jesus sitting on the dashboard of my car, dressed in colors pink and pleasant, glows in the dark 'coz it's iridescent, take it with you when you travel far. Get yourself a sweet madonna, dressed in rhinestone, sitting on a pedestal of abalone shell, goin' on ninety but I ain't scary, coz I know I got the virgin Mary assuring me that I won't go to hell'.

All right, it may be true that as a singer Paul Newman makes a great salad dressing, but to anyone who has done time, it means something. If they've seen it, that is.

I've got the first verse of that song tattooed on my lower back and

I guess it's safe to say that it is my favorite movie of all time. I will have to speak to the bloke who gets the videos for the prison and get him to lift his game. Anyone who hasn't seen that old classic should hang his head. There was the great scene where Luke tried to eat a huge amount of boiled eggs for a bet. These health conscious days if they made a remake they'd cut that scene because of cholesterol levels. The new flick would have a rough, tough crim gobbling down tofu or lentil burgers.

The number of young blokes who have not only never read the works of the great Banjo Paterson and Henry Lawson, but haven't even heard of them, is quite sad and amazing. These aren't fresh off the boat Vietnamese, these are fifth, sixth, seventh and eighth generation Aussie kids – Tasmanians whose family heritage goes back to the early convict days.

I mean these are fair dinkum 'She'll be sweet mate' bloody Aussies, and they've never heard of 'Waltzing Matilda'. Some of the young crims here think culture is something you make yogurt with. They believe they can learn about Asian history by watching Ninja Turtles. They think Henry Lawson bowled for Australia, and Banjo Paterson's is a theatre restaurant in Adelaide.

Can you believe that? Yet the same young men know the words off by heart to half the songs AC/DC ever wrote.

Who was it who wrote *Poor Fellow My Country?* Xavier Herbert? Well, he wasn't far wrong, was he?

The Americanisation of Australia seems to be the problem. The Yanks killed Phar Lap and Les Darcy and they have been trying to kill off everything Australian ever since. The buggers have nearly done it and I'm just as bloody guilty as everyone else for falling victim to it.

This country has a great history and yet you wouldn't know it. The kids walk around with baseball hats on, shirts with gridiron teams' emblems on the front. They have pictures of American basketballers on their walls. They think Chips Rafferty invented the potato cake.

We look up to Yankeeland heroes and look down on our own. It makes me bloody sick. Too much bloody television, if you ask me. It's killing us all. Kids should not be indoors watching television, they should be outside, punching on with their mates, getting a bit of fresh air and doing a bit of male bonding.

Mind you, my distaste for America does not include Gary Cooper, John Wayne, Paul Newman and Edward G. Robinson. God Bless them all, the dirty rats.

ONE of my pet hates is the way Aussie country music has gone. These boys and girls make me cringe with embarrassment when they bung on accents like they were brought up in Mississippi. It is yet another case of the Americanisation of Australia.

You get truck drivers from Nowra who sing like Willie Nelson. You get cowgirls from Queensland who sound like they were brought up in Dallas.

YANKEE DOODLE AUSSIE

Yeah, they call it Aussie music,
With their Mississippi twang,
Singing down home Yankee songs,
With a touch of Aussie slang,
They sold out to Waylon Jennings ,
And sing Rockabilly Blue,
But what they all forget
Is that Aussie land has its legends too,
Yeah, I know Tex Morton's dead,
And his songs are getting rusty,
But there's one Aussie Boy who won't die,
A legend named Slim Dusty,
And what about Banjo Paterson,
And a bloke named Henry Lawson,

Old Flash is dead and gone,
But we've still got Smokey Dawson,
They get up there to Tamworth,
With their Texas hats and bash,
But as far as I'm concerned,
They can jam their Johnny Cash,
Give me Waltzing Matilda,
And the Road to Gundagai,
Hell, I'd rather hear Chad Morgan scream,
Than Willie Nelson cry,
Did you know that Hank Williams died,
With a needle up his arm,
He was just a southern junkie,
And a long way from the farm,
So if you want to sing Aussie country,
And become a legend too,
Forget the Yankee Doodle shit,
And stick to Old True Blue.

THE day I hear Slim Dusty sing the American national anthem is they day I'll get a rope and a chair and hang myself.

I don't know whether to laugh or cry. I have just attended what is called a poetry workshop conducted by a noted Australian poet and author, Dorothy Porter, bless her heart. She put us through a somewhat spaced-out semi-psychological trip into the world of the modern poet.

Apparently Lawson and Paterson are yesterday's men, swept aside with the wave of an academic hand. The poets of today seem to be taken with the autumn leaf that fell to the ground while the author sits on top of the fridge crying tears that belong to the next door neighbor's goldfish, all to the tune of one hand clapping.

Perish the thought that anyone should write a poem that actually rhymes. Miss Porter was much taken with the Japanese style of poetry called 'haiku'. Yes, that's what Aussie land needs, a little more Japanese culture jammed down our simple literary necks.

I read a poem to Miss Porter. It went down like a fart in church. I don't know haiku, I like my fish cooked, I eat red meat and I drink my coffee out of a mug, not a glass, so I will never be considered a trendy. But one thing I know, and that is that my poems rhyme.

These government grant authors and poets may think of me as some dumb bar-room story teller, but I think some of them are 'Beam me up Scottie' space cadets. Some of these people seem to think if it comes from Australia it must be crap. As far as I am concerned give me the local product every time.

Miss Porter may be all the rage in the sushi bar set, but I reckon I'm not too bad when it comes to a bit of Aussie-style poetry. You be the judge. Here's a couple, one about my old mate, the former Chief Magistrate of Victoria, Darcy Dugan, and the other about Supreme Court judge and head of the parole board Frank 'The Tank' Vincent.

DARCY

He sat on the bench,
For many years,
He gave us laughs,
And sometimes tears,
He had a way,
All his own,
And for style,
He stood alone,
With smiling face,
And big bowtie,
My word, he did look classy,
Every crook in Melbourne knew him,
The Magistrate called Darcy.

BIG FRANK

For classic courtroom comedy,
In Australia we are not short,
And the funniest of them all,
Sits in a Melbourne Court,
The Mick Irish son of a tough old dockie,
Heart of gold, but his head's a little rocky,
The Chairman of the Board,
As every crook will know,
They tried to pull his coat,
But he still let the Texan go,
He hits 'em in the courtroom,
Like an Irish tank,
The knockabout Judge,
They all call Big Frank.

EVERY now and again the jail allows concerts. The last show the prison put on was a South African bongo player and it went down like a turd in a punch bowl. What this jail needs is what Pentridge put on in the early 70s – a strip show with a professional stripper. I happen to know several professional strippers who would be only too pleased to come into the jail and put on a properly-run show for no charge whatsoever.

Any inmate wishing to attend the event could cough up $5 and all the money could be given to the prison sports and recreation fund. You'd get at least a hundred prisoners wishing to attend, it would be a fun night out and a good little earner.

It would also lead to prisoners making a great effort to behave in jail. They would remember what pussy looked like and would be on their best behaviour to get out as soon as possible.

'Alexandra the great 48' nearly caused a riot in B Division in Pentridge when she put on a show. But when the South African bongo player showed up at the Pink Palace only about seven inmates bothered to attend. At least a properly run and tasteful strip show would encourage prisoner interest.

If we do happen to get a few strippers into the jail, they won't miss me. I'll be the bloke in the front row looking as flash as a rat with a gold tooth. Two gold teeth, in fact, and that's not all. In September Dr Carlton, the prison dentist, fitted me with my new super duper cobalt chrome false teeth, which include two solid gold teeth in front. I've had them in ever since. They fit a treat and my smile is the envy of the prison, with every crook in the jail with teeth missing – and there's a few – now wanting to invest in a cobalt chrome denture with gold teeth as an optional extra.

Ahh, Chopper, you old trend setter. But as I said to the boys, if you really want to look like the Chopper, get them bloody ears off. The mention of the razor blade slicing through the ears soon separates the men from the boys.

MY young legal advisers Peter Warmbrunn and Anita Valentine come in to see me occasionally. Painless Pete is turning into a bonny courtroom buccaneer, and Anita Valentine is well-named: my heart skips a beat whenever I see her. I've promised to toss a nice murder case her way some time in the future, when she feels herself ready for the big one.

I tossed Anita Betts a nice case in the form of the Amanda Carter murder mystery – a 13-year-old mystery and probably the biggest murder case in Tasmania this century. The accused sought my advice regarding legal help when he came into the remand yard in 1993 and I promptly advised him to forget all others and hire Anita Betts. I'm sure I can muster up a nice little murder case for young Anita Valentine when she is ready to rock and roll. That reminds me. I must toss a murder case to Peter Warmbrunn next time a nice little stabbing or shooting or acid bath killer jumps up.

My wise old legal adviser and courtroom chess player Mr Pat (God

Bless Him) Harvey, the solicitor who helped save my neck in the 'Sammy the Turk' murder case, once said to me: 'Chopper, a criminal lawyer's reputation is made or broken in the remand yard of a prison.'

That advice I passed on to Anita Betts, and she in turn to Peter Warmbrunn, and he in turn passed these words of wisdom to the lovely Miss Valentine. Meaning that Anita Betts and her legal firm practically live in the remand yard at Risdon, visiting clients, and have grown into the strongest legal firm in Tasmania. While all around them, most of the other lawyers in town are starving to death. Ha ha.

The so-called big name lawyers in Tassie prior to my arrival in the state have sunk like the Titanic. They were big ships once, but they are all at the bottom of the sea now. Why? Because criminals decide who the best criminal lawyers are ... a small point that lawyers forget. If I stand on the muster line in front of the whole yard and I'm asked by a young bloke in trouble: 'Hey, Chopper, I've got Mr So-and-so as my lawyer, what do you reckon of him?', and I spit on the ground and say 'sack the bum, he's a rat and you can't trust him', then I'm afraid that's one sacked lawyer.

You need more than a legal degree to be a lawyer. You need to care, because you're dealing with men and women in trouble. Guilty or innocent, these poor buggers are at their wits' end. Some are on the edge of suicide or, at best, a nervous breakdown.

The remand yard of a prison is a cold and lonely place, and your lawyer for that period in your life is your only true friend, and my advice to any who seek it, is to pick your friends wisely.

CHAPTER 21

BLACK HUMOUR, WHITE DEATHS IN CUSTODY

THE more I see the way poor old Aussieland is going the madder I become. I grew up as a good little racist under the white Australia policy and like every other red-blooded Aussie kid of that era, enjoyed putting a goodly bit of comical shit on the Abos, spooks, coons, slopes, chows, dagos, spags, spics, greasers and wogs – and whatever other third world gin jockey or porch monkey that came along. And what bloody good fun it was.

Yet the same Aussie kids would put shit on the Germans for what they did to the Jews and we always enjoyed hating the filthy Japs for what they did to the Diggers during the Second World War.

We all grew up racist but we picked and chose. There were exceptions and contradictions to our racist rules and all in the name of fun. We would put shit on the Abos, yet jump to their defence if any outsider such as some wog tried to put shit on what was after all the real Australian. We were, and still are, a confused lot of buggers indeed.

Australia has no religious hatreds apart from the fact that

everyone's Dad was either a Catholic or a Freemason. We would happily put shit on every wog in town, except of course for the Italian and Greek kids we classed as our friends, because they weren't wogs, they were our mates.

The wogs were the buggers from the next suburb we fought with on Saturday night.

As far as our racist attitudes went we invented the rules as we went along, making exceptions for friends and allowing all sorts of contradictions to our elastic rules.

I guess you could say that our racist attitude was a rule of law that we applied nine out of ten times. Sporting identities, boxers, footy players and wog chicks with big tits were the general exceptions, and our friends of the non-Australian variety.

What a confused bunch of two-faced racists we were and still are. But the rising wave of nutters and neo-Nazi groups have tossed new cards into our old relaxed deck. These buggers hate everybody, the blacks, Asians, the wogs, the Left wingers, the greenies, the Catholics, the Jews, and the Freemasons. They say they hate the homosexuals, yet Nazi history is littered with rampant homosexuals. The head of Hitlers 'brown shirts', Ernst Rohm, was as 'camp as a row of mein tents'. Adolf Hitler's maternal grandmother was a Jew, so to was the maternal grandmother of Heinrich Himmler's righthand man, S.S. Oberfuhrer 'General' Reinhard Heydrich.

In fact, when one checks the family histories and sexual taste of the world's leading Nazis you'll find shady blood lines and freckle punchers littering their ranks. The big Nazi rallies should be part of Sydney's gay mardi gras – they would be at home there.

The whole thing is bunghole rubbish. The neo-Nazis in Germany today hate the Turks, yet the Turks backed Germany in the First World War and backed Hitler in the Second World War.

Shocking punters the Turks: two bets for two losses. I agree that the influx of Vietnamese and other Asian peoples to Australia today is creating big social problems and a lot of jealousy and resentment and for good reason. The poor old Aussie feels like a stranger in his own country, but waving swastikas and joining the ranks of the neo-Nazis is not the way to go.

In Pentridge we created a joke version of the Ku Klux Klan, but the whole thing was a giggle. I was wearing a pillow case, standing next to two prison officers. Some said it improved my looks. Foul slander, I say.

But the whole racial question is getting out of hand and I believe it is a serious problem. I believe that everything will sort itself out in time. But the neo-Nazis see the Aussies' natural dislike of outsiders as a tool to be used to get the average Australian to agree with the Nazis on the Asian question. They would then argue, 'You must also agree that the Jews must go as well, the Catholic church, and the Freemasons'. The list is endless.

It's nonsense, but very dangerous nonsense.

SPEAKING of growing up with wogs, it was with some amusement that I noted the arrest of Trevor Pettingill along with a Calabrian gentleman on charges relating to two crops from a marijuana plantation near Driffield, wherever the hell Driffield is. *(Near Sale in Gippsland – ed.)*

The arrest of Pettingill is a small change matter. In my opinion he is and will always remain a two-bob nothing little punk in a posh suit his mummy bought him, in spite of his acquittal along with others in the Walsh Street shootings. What interests and amazes me is that his co-accused was not only a Calabrian, but one whose family I think I grew up with in the northern suburbs. If it is the same family, they were a very large and respected Italian family indeed, and it surprises me that any member of it might associate with low-rent rubbish like Trevor Pettingill. I went to school in Thomastown with a family of Calabrians, fought alongside them in street battles and remember them with fondness. This particular family were very closeknit and respected, but Thomastown in those days was a Sicilian stronghold, and the Sicilians always had the whip hand. I remember having a punch on with one of the Calabrian boys and being set upon by various of his relatives, only to be rescued by a guy called 'Teacup' Tommy with a few simple words spoken in his thick Sicilian accent.

I didn't understand Italian too well then, although I ended up being able to speak it well enough to make myself understood. But, I believe Tommy's words related to killing their mother if they continued to hit me.

Sicilians, Tommy always told me, took no nonsense from Calabrians. The big Italian crime families in Australia are all of Calabrian blood. However, as Tommy and my old mate 'Poppa' told me, the Calabrians run it all because the Sicilians allow them to do so. That's how it works in Italy, and that's how it works here.

Any Calabrian family which wishes to operate in certain areas of interest without the nodding approval of the Sicilians could very well find themselves lying dead beside a river with their ears cut off. But that, as they say in the classics, is another story.

The newspapers and TV are full of mafia this and mafia that, but the Calabrian crime families are not mafia. The Sicilians are the true mafia, and the Calabrians operate on a sort of licence from them. I've seen fully grown 40 and 50-year-old hard Calabrian men cross the road and walk on the other side to avoid 'Teacup' Tommy and Little Mario, who were only teenage tough kids, because the Sicilians represented what the Calabrians only pretended to be. 'Teacup' would always spit on the ground when walking past a Calabrian in Thomastown, and fully-grown men would cop this sweet and walk on. The structure of the Italian crime world and families was explained to me at an early age, and I've taken a keen interest in it ever since.

All I can say is that Trevor 'small change' Pettingill will want to pray to God that it wasn't his fault that the Calabrian got pinched with him, as the families I knew would eat the Pettingills for Sunday lunch. The Calabrians are without question the leading organised crime power in Australia, as they operate with the full approval of their Sicilian 'masters'. However, as I've mentioned in my other books, there is a situation unique in Melbourne, and that is the horrific reputation of one small ethnic group whose presence maintains a peaceful balance of power. And that is the Albanians. The Albanian mafia and its thirst for revenge and bloodshed not only keeps the Calabrians in check, but the Sicilians don't particularly want to go out of their way to upset them either. Ha ha.

In 1987 a crew of Calabrians swore to kill me, but my simple friendship with two Albanian gentlemen prevented the Calabrians from moving against me in force. These two gentlemen were not criminals. Perish the thought. However, I owe my life to old Norm Dardovski and young Neville, as had any Calabrian bullet fired at me accidentally hit one of the Dardovski family the Albanians would have drowned the offenders and every relative they had in a river of blood. The loyalty and friendship of the Dardovski family is something I will never forget.

Now we watch TV and, as I predicted years ago, we see the Vietnamese flexing their muscles. The Chinese, in the form of the 14K, are long established and going peacefully about their business, but the Vietnamese aim to overtake them, and from there they will team up with or overtake the Italians. Then, in ten years or less, they will run into the Albanians. Then you'll find Vietnamese popping up all over the place as dead as doornails. Ha ha.

The Sicilians will threaten to kill your mother. The Vietnamese really will kill your mother. However, the Albanian mafia will actually not only kill your mother but put the body in the cooking pot. The KGB didn't use the Albanians as hitmen for nothing. Next to the Irish, they would be the greatest mental cases in the criminal world. Forgive my raving on, but the recent drive-by shooting death of John Newman, the MP in NSW, has again triggered my thoughts about the Vietnamese and the ladder I can see them climbing.

What the Viets forget is that they all come from large families –

meaning they can be 'got at'. The Viets will kill your family. The Albanians will revenge tenfold – and the Irish-Aussie criminal gets a bit puzzled by it all, and will run around half full of Irish whiskey and shoot rapid fire at anything that looks sideways at him from a distance of 300 yards. In the criminal wars, the smartest get the cash, but the maddest get the victory, and Aussie-Irish-Scottish-English old school crook has yet to meet his equal, which fills my heart with a certain joy. As while the wogs and rice eaters battle it out, the Aussie old school still rule. As (Linus Patrick) Driscoll once said, there's no mafia in Belfast. An attitude which means that the Aussie crook will never be beaten in his own land. Ha ha. Thank God.

BACK in the middle of June another bright spark took early parole. He hanged himself ten minutes before lunch. We had Chiko rolls too. Yummy. I've heard of food critics but that's bloody ridiculous.

I shouldn't laugh at the despair of others, but it's a sort of sad laughter. Poor bastards.

That's the second hanging in six weeks. Good thing they weren't black or all hell would break loose. White fellas are stringing themselves up and slashing their wrists and necks in jails and police lockups all over Australia and as soon as an Abo does it the Prime Minister gets a phone call.

The poor old white fellas in custody are going down like tent pegs and no bugger says a word, but when Truganini's great grandson takes a nose dive off the top landing suddenly it's a day of national mourning.

What about the poor white kids? I guess that bit of sarcasm is in bad taste, but it is true the white deaths in custody far outweigh the black deaths yet no one ever seems to notice the poor buggers unless they are of Aboriginal descent.

The whole topic of suicide in prison, or police stations is sad and depressing and it puts you in a very solemn frame of mind. If you don't have a bit of a black comedy – sorry, dark comedy – you soon become depressed.

The whole thing is very sad but you can't legislate against suicide. Of all the living things man is the only one who commits suicide so it must be part of our nature.

TASMANIA is the land of the snow white Abo. When I first got to Risdon Prison one of the first questions I was asked was did I claim Aboriginal descent. Had I done so the Aboriginal legal aid service would have funded my legal case, or so I was told.

All anyone has to do down here is claim Aboriginal descent to be classed as an Aboriginal, and then you can claim and get all manner of wonders bestowed upon you. While there are quite a few real true blue Abos in Tassie and they are good blokes too, the ones I've met, there are three times as many who are so white, blue-eyed and blonde that they look like members of the bloomin' Nazi party.

But because their great great grandfathers once waved at Truganini from a distance of 300 yards they claim Aboriginal descent and jump on the gravy train.

If you have feathers and webbed feet, if you swim in water and go quack, quack and look like a duck then it's a safe bet you're a bloody duck, it doesn't matter if your great, great grandfather was a bloody budgie. If you have white skin and blonde or red hair or any color hair, for that matter, then you're white. It's no use trying to say you're a black man.

For crying out loud, my great granny was Chinese, my dear old Dad is quarter caste Chinese, but that don't mean that I can walk up to the Chinese Embassy and say 'give us a bloody passport'. The Chinese side of the family came to Australia during the gold rush days but that don't make me a Chinaman, for God's sake.

(Speaking of this, a distant cousin wrote to me to inform me that my Chinese great grandmother I mentioned in my first book was not the only Chinese connection in my family tree. There was a great, great grand father named Cheong Shin Hun on my Grandfather's side of the family. It is all quite confusing, but it seems there is

Chinese blood on both sides of my Dad's family. Cheong Shin Hun probably means 'hand over the money, slanty eyes.' Maybe I should be called 'Chopsticks' Read.)

With my family Chinese connection, should I pull up on the Asian jokes? I think not.

The other side of the clan is Irish, but that don't make me a bloody leprechaun, either. I'm an Aussie, a white man with a teaspoon full of 'Fu Manchu' in my bloodline. Big deal. But there is so much to be gained from the state and federal governments if you claim Aboriginal descent and are smart and know how to play the system that a lot of white people are jumping on the gravy train.

All a sixteen-year-old unmarried mother has to do is tell the hospital that her new born baby's father is an Aboriginal and she and the baby are sweet.

I reckon the Aussie Abo is a good bloke and good luck to him. It's these white false pretenders that create all the trouble. I'm not dirty on the poor old dinky di Abos. I don't think any Aussie is, but I am a bit dirty on the snow white 'Koorie' fakes who on the strength of nothing, or a teaspoon of Aboriginal blood a hundred years back, expect the Aussie taxpayer to wipe their backsides for them for the rest of their lives. The whole thing has gotten out of hand. The whiter they get the more they bloody want. They're as bad as the bloody public servants.

I mean, us poor old Chinese Irishmen don't get any free goodies, so why should they?

I better go now. I feel like a pint of Guinness and some fried rice.

CHAPTER 22

WHY I'M NOT A FATHER

I HAVE been carrying on a lengthy debate for some time now with a lady friend of mine, Margaret Hamilton. She is the Margaret in my life I never mentioned before. She is a mother of three and a good friend of mine and Robert Lochrie.

The debate is why I have never been, or allowed myself to be the father of children. A totally outrageous thought, if you ask me. Yet female friends of mine insist that I would make a wonderful Dad. The debate has gone on and on with me losing ground and big Margaret's arguments holding fast.

I then got a phone call from Anita and she told me that the High Court rejected my leave to appeal. So that is that, a perfect argument for why I've never been a Dad.

My life is a never-ending nightmare. I wouldn't want to be a part-time father. The idea of my kids coming to see me in jail would be too cruel to everybody. I have chosen my life, I am what I am, but how could I inflict it on children?

As for my little mate Tauree (whose last name is Cleaver, a name that somewhat amuses me considering my name) she'd make a good getting-out-of-jail present ... except that by then we both could have grey hair, glasses, false teeth, hearing aids and walking sticks! But it was a happy thought while it lasted. Mary-Ann of course is in tears and in all honesty if I had a tear to cry I'd be bawling my eyes out now. How long is a piece of string? Well, that's how long I will have to do in jail, held at the Governor's pleasure.

It is so hard to live with no light at the end of the tunnel. So now I will set about petitioning the Governor of the state of Tasmania. I'll petition him so much he will have nightmares about me. He'll get so much mail I will become a life patron to Aussie Post.

IN the past any shooting matter where the victim lived, it was a simple Magistrates' Court matter and a two year sentence, but in Tassie it is the twelfth of never and for the only one I did not do.

This has to be the sins of my past come back to get me. So Damian Bugg and Sid have finally beat me, or have they?

The sad part to all this is that it will probably finish my old Dad. I doubt that he will live long enough for me to ever see him again, face to face as a free man. Anita Betts told me that Mr David Porter put up a sterling effort, as I'm sure he did. Tauree once wrote to me, 'Chopper, do you think they held your books against you?' and went on to say that she thought that if my name was not Chopper Read I would have won my court case in the beginning.

Out of the mouths of babes many true things are said and I have all the time in the world to wonder about that particular line of thought. Meanwhile I'm still smiling away like the joker gone mad.

It may not be justice, but I guess it is a bitter and twisted form of poetic justice. Oh well. They got me for the wrong crime but I'm no clean skin.

SPEAKING of Dad, he is getting sicker and stranger by the month, and I feel powerless to help him in here.

The last time I saw him was when Micky Marlow brought him down to see me. These days I cannot tell him a thing for fear he stands in the street and blabs it to the neighbors and passers-by.

It is very sad for me to read his letters these days as I can no longer understand a word he is on about. It is a strange feeling; he is alive but I've lost him. I can see him clearly in my memory, but when he visited me last he was a faded shadow of the man I knew and, mentally, he was no longer my father.

Dad was always a funny piece of work. In 1977 when we were living together in Rockley Road, South Yarra, I would get ready to go out at night. While I would shower and shave Dad would lay all my clothes out for me after he ironed and pressed everything.

I would dress and put on my overcoat, a beautiful old black box Chester overcoat, and then I'd say to Dad 'Where is my shotgun?' and he would run off and come back with my sawn-off 12-gauge shotgun. I would say 'ammo' and he'd say 'bird shot or SGs?' and he would come back with half a dozen assorted shells. I would say 'Where is my cut throat razor?' and off he would go to fetch my razor and I'd yell out 'My pliers as well' and he would yell back, 'Will you need your knuckle buster?' He always called the knuckle duster the 'buster'. Anyway, this comedy would go on until I was fully armed.

Then, as I was ready to leave, I would give Dad a kiss on the cheek and a hug and he would pat me on the back and say 'Okay son, you can't be too careful in your line of business. Don't get into any trouble'. Ha ha. There I am going out the door at midnight with enough cold steel and firepower to fight off a small invading army and my old Dad is telling me not to get into any trouble.

I remember after I shot a crook called Johnny in 1977 I accidentally left the spent cartridge near the scene of the crime and I got my Dad to drive me back to look for it. Lucky for me I found it. I ended up getting two years jail over that at a later date, and my Dad gave me a lecture all the way home in the car. 'You should have taken his head off, son. Bloody shooting these bums in the legs is no good. You are not running a public charity.' To which I'd be saying: 'Yes Dad, no Dad, I'm sorry Dad.'

'You bloody knucklehead', he would call me. Now he cannot even recall the event. It is a sad and terrible thing to watch someone you love fade away. Micky Marlow pops in to see Dad now and again. Dad relates stories of being spied on by neighbors and police and plots and plans afoot aimed at him by the forces of evil, all of it somehow relating to me. If the handle comes off the teacup then it's a case of sabotage by unseen enemies. I receive letters of violent outrage from him ranting and raving at me over things that make no sense to me at all. Then at other times he writes to me in his old loving manner.

Stuck in here I do worry about the old fellow and his wellbeing. Years ago while Dad was making us a cup of Milo in the kitchen, me and Dave the Jew sat in the lounge room cleaning a pump action shotgun, and Dave said in a whisper, 'Your Dad isn't making Milo again, is he? He nearly killed me with the last cup he made.'

Dad was putting laxatives into Dave's Milo. He would stand there and force Dave to drink the Milo. Dave the Jew loved my Dad, but Dave always felt that my old Dad was madder than he was. Ha ha.

Dave now lives alone with his old Dad and I know he hopes that when our fathers pass away that the two of us will live together. My greatest fear is that my Dad will pass away while I'm in jail.

CHAPTER 23

HOW THE 'LEOPARD' GOT SPOTTED

I'VE just spent nearly half an hour rolling around my cell floor laughing my head off. It is heart warming to hear that the boys from the old neighborhood are still rocking and rolling. I have just heard the Victorian police swept up nine of them in a drug operation.

It couldn't have happened to a nicer group of clowns. Two of them have quite decent priors, The 'Leopard' and The Greek. Oh well, you can't put bow ties on billy goats. Those numb nuts insist on getting around with the bloody Greek and then wonder why they come undone. The Greek's idea of keeping a secret is to tell 1000 prostitutes everything he knows and then pray to God that they will all keep their mouths shut.

But the big shock in all of this is The 'Leopard'. I was always of the personal belief that he would never see the inside of a prison. Some unkind people have suggested to me that he is in fact the drug boss I wrote about in my first book. Well, I'm afraid that I will have to adopt the same attitude and policy as the American Navy, and neither confirm nor deny.

The last time I saw 'Leopard' we had our photo taken together at a party at The Greek's place. Mad Charlie took the photo. Gonzo was there. Neville the Albanian, Jungle Jim, Mad Archie, Big Mick, Black Boris, Scottish Steve, various Italian gentleman and Shane Goodfellow.

'Leopard' arrived with a small army of bodyguards and hangers on. Half the people at the party either wanted to shoot the other half or were plotting to do so. We had kidnapped a stripper and cage dancer from Bojangles, a beautiful little Greek girl named Nicole, who has stuck loyal to me ever since I saved her from being raped.

She's a beautiful little chick and a good kid. I started to play Russian roulette and the party soon broke up. We ended up at the Chevron with little Nicole doing a strip on top of the grand piano. Who said we were not cultured?

In the piano bar a small fight broke out and we ended up outside the nightclub. Guns were produced and shots fired. No-one was hurt. We were all too drunk to hit the side of a barn with a shovel of wheat. I gave my gun to Nicole to hold for me and went to the airport and flew back to Tassie. Enough fun for one night. Harmless male bonding, I call it.

I always liked 'Leopard', even though he was involved in an area of crime that I loathed. He had brains, and in a strange way I had a sneaking regard for his thinking ability.

I knew that maybe one day I'd kill him, or maybe he would have me killed, but in spite of all that I always found him to be a likeable fellow. He was one Mr Big who made a profession of acting like a Mr Small, but he was ten times bigger than even his friends and business colleagues could ever imagine.

He was a highly-skilled tactician and criminal puppet master. Rumors over the past 12 months, even longer, have been getting about that both the Greek and the 'Leopard' have both been kidnapped by the heroin and speed needle.

I can't vouch for the truth of that but it would explain how

'Leopard' got arrested and his mixing in such low-rent business circles. In 1987 he could have bought or sold every crook in the western suburbs out of petty cash.

Oh well, what can you say. You can't expect people to pull their socks up if they are only wearing thongs. Ha ha.

CHAPTER 24

OH WELL, THERE GOES THE WOMEN'S MARKET

WITHIN weeks of the release of my third book the letters of outrage from female readers started to flood in. I sincerely hope a competent secretary is locked up in Risdon soon to help me answer all this mail.

The letters ask how dare I be unfaithful to little Margaret, how dare I refer to girls as a penny a truck load, how dare I accuse prostitutes of being incapable of love, how dare I say this and how dare I say that.

They say Chopper Read is a woman hater and that they hope I lose my appeal, that I'm an animal, insane, have no regard for the feelings of any women, and so on.

The point is that my feelings towards women are the same as my feelings towards men. I've met some fantastic ones and I've found some diamonds in my life, but in general they are a steaming great shower of shit that I wouldn't piss on. As a rule, if the female of the species did not provide a sexual advantage, the male of the species wouldn't even engage the buggers in conversation.

Call me old-fashioned.

The trouble is if I was to write sweet-tasting lies the stupid buggers would lap it up and love it, but tell the truth and they will hate you forever. I've got a small army of friends, both male and female, and as long as I'm sweet with the people I love and who love me then what the rest of the human race thinks is of no importance.

People buy my books at $12.95 a pop, the same price as a counter lunch and two pots of beer, and feel that they know me well enough to judge me. They take pen in hand and proceed to pour out their personal venom and critical judgment of my life. The mad buggers certainly ask a lot for their $12.95.

Speaking of the diamonds among my women friends, I got a wonderful letter from little Margaret. In it she made a touching comment that I thought I'd share with you. She said: 'Would you believe that I do stupid things like going down to the South Melbourne beach when I'm feeling down? I sit there and I look over the horizon and I can see you waving at me and I then feel good that I had that moment with you. I'm an old sook aren't I?'

She went on to say she will love me until the day she dies and continue to love me after that. I'm afraid her letter brought a slight dampness to the eye. Old Billy 'The Texan' Longley was reading the poem I wrote for little Margaret out to her over the phone, as he had my third book before she could get a copy. He broke into a sob half way through the poem and had to hang up. It must be the crying season.

Anita Betts hasn't even come into see me yet as she is so upset and tearful. Mary-Ann is having a crying fit, Karen the White Dove is in tears. Nicole Sutorius and Big Margaret Hamilton were on the phone to the jail crying and letters of tears and sympathy are coming in fast; not a dry eye in the house.

AFTER a lifetime of study, I have come up with what I believe to be a rock solid doctrine on the vexing topic of the female of the species, and it would be selfish of me not to share it.

I see all females without exception as suffering from a mental and emotional psychosis that I call 'the schizophrenic condition'. It isn't their fault; it's just the way it is. They tend to be insecure, afraid, puzzled, confused, worried, concerned, ill at ease and lacking self-esteem and self-confidence. Not only that, they are dizzy, scatty, flighty, totally withdrawn from reality and tend to totally distort of reality. And loving, hateful, possessive, jealous, greedy, generous, dreamers and fantasy merchants living in a world of romantic imagination.

A bit like members of the Democrats.

Yep, they have a list of mental and emotional disorders a mile long, all on the boil. Add the sex and motherhood urge to this and you have a totally neurotic, obsessional, anxious, head banging, raving, ranting nut case of the highest and most dangerous order.

In other words the classic schizophrenic condition. We are talking about human beings who undergo 12 separate mood swings every 12 hours.

Most men are basically suffering from what I call the 'psychopathic condition'. And if you walk into the day room of any mental hospital in any country you'll find one psychopath standing in the middle of the room surrounded by a dozen schizophrenics hanging on his every word. This is why men can attract and control women.

The imagination of every female secretly longs for the knight in shining armor to ride up on his snow white charger and dry her tears, sweep her off her feet and gallop off into the sunset.

Every schizophrenic basically wants to burst into tears and bury himself in the strong protecting arms of a friend. Of the two, men do the laughing, women do the crying. The psychopath is given to laughter in the face of any and all situations. The schizophrenic is given to tears. All females also suffer from what I call the 'Mills and Boon' nightmare that all women long for and all men laugh at.

To control the mental and emotional being of the classic schizophrenic you must capture their imagination. Paint them a picture and show them the picture and tell them it's theirs.

In handling the schizophrenic condition you must humor it, flatter it, amuse it, and baffle it with bullshit. You must treat it as you would a playful, wilful, crying, spoilt, little child and lower your own intelligence to the same wave length.

The game played between men and women is akin to the role of doctor and patient. How true is that rough old Aussie saying 'that if they never had a snatch we wouldn't even talk to the bastards'.

Mind you, I hope you don't think that my attitude toward females means that I hate women. I love them. They are beautiful, magical and fascinating creatures and it's just that I view both male and females as suffering from two forms of mental and emotional psychosis.

In a sense, I see all men as killers and all women as whores. Not all men are physical killers, of course. Only a small percentage of the male population will actually kill, but all men carry a very strong killer instinct within them.

And not all women are whores, but the whore instinct is within every woman. We all know in our hearts that this is true no matter how much we may deny it. In fact, denying the unpleasant truth to ourselves is all part of the general insanity that goes to make up the human condition.

If you mentally and emotionally tickle a man in the right or wrong place, depending on how you view it, he will kill. Tickle a women in the right place and she will whore her arse to the Devil, and love it as she hates herself doing it.

Homosexual people are the reverse. The homosexual man has the whore instinct within him and the lesbian woman has the killer instinct within her, making the lesbian woman possibly the most mentally and emotionally dangerous of all human creatures ... a schizophrenic psychopath. Mind boggling.

I've said that the schizophrenic condition is a classic female condition. In my opinion most male schizophrenics are either homosexual or bisexual and the ones who are neither homosexual or bisexual are not suffering from the classic schizophrenic condition

203

but from a simple paranoid psychosis and an over-active imagination incorrectly treated by the guesswork warriors of medical science.

Of course, most people would rather dismiss me as a ranting mental case than admit that what I'm saying has an alarming ring of truth to it.

The psychopath condition of the male will fade and grow weak with age but never quite vanish. The schizophrenic condition of the female will remain strong within her until she is 25 to 30 years of age then fade and vanish with her looks.

This is probably one of the main reasons why I've never allowed myself to father children. How could I in all consciousness leave my son or daughter alone in the same room with a schizophrenic? Bad enough having a psychopath for a father without the added insult of a schizophrenic for a mother. Ha ha.

Let's face it. When we were all little kids we looked at our Mums and Dads and we all thought the same thing. 'Jesus Christ, look at these bastards, they are off their heads'. Ha ha.

Don't let this make you think that my conduct toward women in general is anything less than totally correct. As far as women are concerned I live according to my dear old Dad's wise words of wisdom. 'Son, never hit them with a clenched fist and always wipe the neck of the bottle before offering them a drink'.

I HAVE often been accused 'in jest' of attracting a particular sort of female in the form of the so-called dumb molls, bimbos, the pouting pussy brigade, the stupid cupids, the big, dumb blondes with no brains but all tits and legs. I, on the other hand, have always been very suspicious of the so-called dumb, pouting sexpot. And in spite of making sarcastic, backhand comic remarks about the lack of grey matter between the ears of your average female, I have secretly always believed that in the battle of the sexes that the female has always had the ability to play the male like a fine violin.

I have had a tiptruck load of money removed from my pockets over the years by your so-called 'doodle-shaking dumb bimbo'. Please excuse my use of the American slang word 'bimbo', but the Aussie land equivalent of the bimbo is the word 'moll', and it is a tad bit crude. In my opinion there is no such thing as a dumb blonde or a bimbo. They all play act and are expert in polishing the male ego. I've known some very, very intelligent ladies who specialised in play acting this Marilyn Monroe routine all the way to the bank.

I remember a yarn I heard years ago on this topic. A very famous homosexual movie director in Hollywood told Frank Sinatra that in his opinion Marilyn Monroe was the dumbest bimbo in Hollywood. Sinatra was supposed to have turned to him and with a smile said, 'Ten million bucks in the bank and she's sucking off the Kennedys two at a time. Brother, you should be so dumb.'

Yes, we constantly put shit on them while they walk to the bank with our money. There is absolutely no such thing as a dumb woman, because as soon as a bloke hangs his pants over the end of the bed he leaves his brains in his back pocket, and even though I know this the little buggers get me every time. God bless them. Well, let's just say they used to get me. It took me from my teenage years to nearly 40 years of age to snap out of it.

Now that the little buggers are young enough to be my daughters I can see them coming a mile away. And while every crim in the jail is getting his heart broken by every little doodle shaker in town, I've got Mary-Ann.

There is an old saying, if you're going to get married then marry the girl just like the girl who married dear old Dad. But oh no. What do we do when we are young blokes? We run out and try to find the biggest bangtail bleached blond moll in town and fall in love, and in love, and in love, and from broken heart to broken heart we slowly learn the error of our ways.

I wouldn't go so far as to say that I am totally immune to the hypnotic charms of the 'wiggle when she walks, giggle when she talks', big-eyed, all tits and legs bimbo. I mean, what man is unless he's a poof? But I am making a gallant effort. Ha ha. At least now I can read their minds and have a sly smile to myself, and while other prisoners are slashing their wrists over the conduct of their wiggling, giggling, doodle-shaking girlfriends, I've got Mary-Ann, a good girl. Meaning that in the end, what counts to me is reliability, not razzle dazzle.

AFTER my appeal failed, Mary-Ann came to visit me and told me she would stand by me. I told her she would only break her heart and that it was an impossible situation, but she told me she loved me and would not walk away.

I spoke to little Margaret on the phone and it was a tearful conversation. In spite of some recent bad temper from her in letter to me, it was a loving goodbye phone call.

I have had some bad luck in my time but I have also been blessed when it comes to the female of the species. I have known some women who have been blood loyal and have stuck by me, no matter what sort of mess I have landed in.

The topic of my death came up and I blurted out the fact that anything I've got when I die, or any money from the books, film whatever, anything at all that is mine or is owed to me goes to Margaret in the event of my death as she is the sole beneficiary of my last will and testament.

Well, that broke the phone call up into a tearful fit and almost had me going as well. Whether little Margaret and me are together or not, she will most certainly outlive me and it has to go to someone.

What a depressing topic. My dog, Mr Nibbles, was yapping away in the background. All in all it was a sad phone call. Even though we are no longer together and God knows I put her through hell and did not deserve her, I will always love little Margaret in my heart. No-one can forget ten years. Oh well, what more can I say? That's that. I appear to be doomed to spend the greater part of my adult life in prison. It is not a lifestyle I would recommend.

So if there are kids and teenagers who read my books and think my life sounds as though it has been filled with adventures and fun, forget it. Read my books, have a laugh, then throw them away and forget it.

Don't do what I have done, it is a mess and a one way road to disaster. You cannot take on the world, drug bosses, police, gangsters and the courts. If one doesn't get you, one of the others will.

Go straight, young man. It may sound boring but in the long run, it is the way to go.

CHAPTER 25

MUSINGS ON THE ART OF GUN-SLINGING

WHEN I used to go to the Hobart Supreme Court every day for my two trials and my various appeals, I would always look out the prison van window as we drove down Collins Street. (Hang on, I'll just get up to my window and yell out and ask one of these ratbags what bloody street it is I'm talking about).

Back again – I'm told it is Liverpool street – as we would drive along Liverpool Street we would drive past the Alabama Hotel. I became quite fascinated with the name of this little city pub. I thought to myself that come the day I am shot to death in some wild gun battle, wouldn't it be good if I got blown away in the bar of the Alabama Hotel. I mean can't you just see it in your mind's eye 'Shoot out at the Alabama Hotel'. Ha ha ha.

I've never been in the place in my life and from time to time I see this bloody stupid hotel in my dreams. There is something about the name of this silly little pub that stirs my dramatic instinct.

I've always been a bit of a show pony with a flair for the dramatic, that's what separates criminals who are remembered from the crooks no one ever remembers. The crooks who are remembered by history have a flair for the dramatic. Look at Ned Kelly: you can't tell me that a man who punched two holes in a tin bucket and sticks it on his head hasn't got a natural flair for the dramatic.

So there I was off to court every day looking at this little hotel as we drove past thinking to myself wouldn't that be a great place to be shot to death in and leaving aside the insanity of that sort of thinking you have to admit that it does show a natural flair for the dramatic.

I'm quite taken with the names of some of the pubs in Hobart – The Dog House Hotel, The Errol Flynn Hotel – but you must admit if you had to shoot some bugger or get shot you couldn't go past the 'Alabama Hotel'

One of my American wild west gunslinger heroes was a little known gunman and in spite of the fact that he isn't well remembered by history, his reputation during his lifetime was deadly and feared. His name was Curly Bill Brochus, the master and inventor of a move called the Highwayman's Roll.

It was the sneaky art of taking out your hand gun and handing it, butt first, to the Sheriff or Marshall while a gun was being held on you, in other words the law had got the drop on you and you were handing your weapon over and in a lightning flash and with a flick of the wrist Curly Bill Brochus would flick that gun, so instead of butt first it would spin around and BANG.

He was the sneakiest gunslinger in the West. A back shooting, dry gulching son of a bitch. Curly Bill Brochus killed more men that Doc Holiday, Wild Bill Hitchcock and Billy the Kid put together.

Curly Bill once rode 300 miles to kill three men in the Red Dog Saloon. I myself would have taken a taxi. Which brings me to a matter of financial concern. If you were a professional killer, could you write off cab fares like that as a tax deduction?

Surely a hit man could claim, guns, bullets and such like as business expenses. It seems only fair. You must agree with me that the Alabama Hotel sounds wonderful. Can't you see yourself with your trusty Colt Peacemaker .45 calibre in hand facing down all comers in a hail of lead and a blaze of glory, in the bar of the Alabama Hotel?

Well, I certainly can! Ha ha. Where's your sense of adventure? Have you no flair for the dramatic? That's the trouble with Australia and Aussies. There's not a lot of imagination going on and very little flair for the dramatic.

No wonder we idolise a bloke who ran around country Victoria with a tin bucket on his head.

CHAPTER 26

WHY FIST FIGHTS DON'T RATE

ONE never-ending topic of conversation within the walls of this place never ceases to amaze me … and that is the childish topic of who can beat who in a fist fight.

I stopped talking about that shit a thousand years ago, but in Risdon it is a topic that keeps coming up. So and so is a good fighter, he can beat so and so in a fight.

I remove myself totally from these nitwit conversations by openly telling one and all that at nearly 40 years of age I'm no longer involving myself in any who-can-beat-who in a fist fight contest, and I readily accept the fact that the jail is full of people who could punch my head in.

Thus, I remove myself and my ego from these insane debates. Who can beat who in a fist fight is a squarehead topic. You never hear it spoken of in the criminal world: no one ever ran around saying watch out for Ned Kelly, he's a bloody good fist fighter, or be careful of Squizzy Taylor he fights like ten men, or look out here comes Billy 'the Texan' Longley, gee he can fight good. Al Capone never had no black belt in karate.

In all my years in Pentridge I never heard the topic spoken of in any seriousness, as it never applied in the world of real life and death.

And if you think this contradicts everything I've written about streetfighters I have known, it doesn't. Credit is always given and given in good grace towards any individual who is an outstanding street fighter but we would give the same credit with good grace to someone who was an outstanding football player, swimmer, runner, boxer or poker player.

But in the true world of criminal 'bang bang you're dead' violence it doesn't matter how well you can fight, or play footy. If your number comes up you are off tap and that is that. Dead as a bloody mackerel, no questions asked.

I keep forgetting that the prison population at Risdon is basically made up of squareheads.

They aren't real criminals, just poor buggers who get into a bit of bother with the police now and then.

Most of them are little better than teenage kids and I guess who can beat who in a fist fight is still a big thing in their little brains. But I really do get sick of listening to this shit.

So far all I've heard these buggers talk about is who can beat who in a fist fight, pinching motor cars and gang banging sheilas.

It's a very young prison. There is only a dozen or so blokes my age and older in the place. And I'm not 40 yet.

CHAPTER 27

POLICE SHOOTINGS

IN SIX years between 1980 and 1986 Victorian police shot dead four people. In the following eight years they killed 28 and another man died seven months after he was shot by police and left a paraplegic. Four police have been killed since 1986 and one was accidentally shot dead during a raid.

Police claim there has been a marked change in attitudes since a car bomb went off outside the Russell Street police station on Easter Thursday, 1986, killing policewoman Angela Taylor.

Police are now more heavily armed and better trained in the use of firearms. They have shown that they are more likely to kill than ever before.

In May 1994 Paul Ronald Skews planned to rob a Melbourne Real Estate Agency with another man, Stephen Raymond Crome.

Skews, who had been released from jail in January after serving $2^1/_2$ years for armed robbery, was suspected of robbing a service station, hitting a suburban jewellers and attempting to rob a butcher.

What Skews didn't know while he was planning his next raid was that he was the subject of an armed robbery investigation, code named 'Short Time'.

Skews told friends he was prepared to shoot it out rather than be arrested and he intended to rob a payroll from one of several factories in Springvale.

When Skews and Crome arrived at the real estate agents, five members of the Special Operations Group were waiting in an unmarked van.

The bandits, wearing balaclavas and gloves, were running into the shop when they were confronted by the police. Police and witnesses said Skews pointed his shotgun at the SOG members.

It was the last thing he ever did.

Four of the five SOG members fired 17 shots from their automatic pump action shotguns. They were hit by at least 12 blasts. Both bandits were dead when they hit the ground. The police were uninjured.

IT'S a Saturday morning as I write this and the cold wind and rain is blowing down and all around. Great sheets of it pouring down on the jail and I am in my cell snug as a Bugg (Damian, QC) in a rug. When it rains on the weekend there is no where else to go but your cell. But when you get there the only thing you read about in the papers or hear on the radio is bloody police shootings.

It seems that whenever I pick up a newspaper these days the good old Victoria Police Force has Swiss cheesed yet another malefactor to kingdom come or bashed the barrel of a .38 calibre police special up the date of some scallywag.

As I write this the great debate in C Yard is the death of Paul Skews, who got blown away with a mate when he was about to commit an armed robbery. Or, as the Victorian police like to politely call it, a tactical arrest in the name of the law, otherwise known as 'Get a bit of this into you'.

You can just imagine it. 'Is the suspect under arrest?' yells a chief inspector. The young policeman looks up from the lifeless corpse and says earnestly, 'he certainly looks like he's under arrest to us, sir.'

Another young policeman gives the corpse a little kick to test it and says, 'yes sir, definitely well under arrest'. The chief inspector walks up to the fallen offender and looking down said 'my goodness, now there's a fine example of a man under arrest'. Ha ha.

Well, that's the comedy of my mind's eye but it's close to the truth. It's all part of the cops and robbers game. I keep telling the boys that it is no use whinging about it, because the Aussie crook took it on his own head to follow the American role model. They all want to be Yankee gangsters. Well, welcome to America, boys.

The crooks set the pace and the trend. The cops simply play follow the leader.

When I grew up all the Aussies looked to England to set the example. All police saw themselves in the same light as Scotland Yard and red blooded true blue Aussie crooks saw themselves in the same light as the East End villains.

Then, in the early 1970s everyone went American mad. All the crims desperately began to follow the insane American role model and the police followed along behind them.

The crims armed up, so the cops armed up. The crims lets rip, so the cops let rip. The only problem was the police let rip with more man power, more fire power and more smarts.

'Unfair, unfair,' cried the crooks. Well, what's unfair? If you want to party on, then rock and roll or piss off out of it. I mean, that's the game isn't it – cops and robbers. You can't complain that you only pulled your weapon out to frighten the policeman and that you weren't really going to use it. If you pull a weapon out on someone to scare them, then you stand a bloody good chance of scaring them into blowing your bloody head off.

Silly bastards. The more crims and nutters who get blown away by police and the more police who get blown away by the crims and nutters, the more paranoid and frightened both sides become.

So welcome to America. It's what Australia wanted, to copy America. But whereas cats have nine lives, copy cats get only one.

I'm gun mad. I love them, but unlike most the crims I've come across, I know how to use them. I also know that it takes me a full two weeks to sight a particular hand gun in and practice with it to the point where I can shoot a beer bottle at 20 to 25 paces and a full month of practice until I can hit six beer bottles at 30 paces, with six shots in six seconds, which I do before I bother carrying that hand gun on me as my personal weapon.

It stands to reason that your average young kid policeman or policewomen should have a far greater skill with a handgun than your average idiot crook or nutter. I also know that in my own heart, regardless of my love for guns, I still hold to the old English tradition.

I don't want to kill a copper. The police don't put you in jail. Bad lawyers put you in jail. An arrest only means a court case and at court the police play little or no role in anything, so when the police say, 'Stop, you're under arrest', it's no big deal. It means I wouldn't kill to stay out of prison, or kill to get out of prison.

You may as well stand me on a street corner and tickle me under the arms with a feather duster for all jail means to me. I've got no doubt that if the police tried a tactical arrest on me and I was armed I'd empty my clip before I died, meaning, 'Here lays Mark Brandon "Chopper" Read: killed by people he didn't know over something that wasn't important.'

All this needless violence is caused by too much television, if you ask me. Bloody Aussie land is going mad, and in my opinion the whole bloomin' country could do with a valium, a good cup of tea and a nice lie down. But the great Victorian police shootings debate rages on, regardless, encouraged by the psychologists and criminologists and the rest of the lounge chair, guesswork warriors are giving their learned thoughts and opinions on the pros and cons of it all.

And what a shower of shit they rain down on us. Raving on about re-enactments and Royal Commissions, and disarming the police.

What a lot of flapdoodle. It's the way the game is played. A point totally forgotten by all is that, probably through no fault of their own, police are being pushed into a situation where they are fast becoming a part of the own problem.

It goes like this. I can foresee the day when some silly kid or squarehead or petty crook will be caught red hot in the act of scallywag misconduct. The policeman or woman will reach for his or her gun and begin to draw it out but the offender panics, gets in first and drops the police officer and lives to get to court, then pleads not guilty to murder on the grounds of self-defence, claiming that when he saw the police officer go for the gun, that he knew he was facing almost certain death.

In that moment of less than the blink of an eye he no longer saw a police officer, but he saw his own death, and the natural human instinct for preservation of life took control and he fired his weapon – not to kill, but to live. And the day will come when such a person will be found not guilty by a jury of good citizens who have grown slightly sceptical of the amount of 'tactical arrests' resulting in deaths.

If that happens, the police will realise that in the eyes of the public they are no longer seen as dragon slayers but as a part of the dragon they are trying to slay. Instead of being the solution to the problem, they will have become half the problem.

Wise men will sit and ask why the attitude of the general public toward the murder of a police officer may no longer be one of all heads bowed for a minute's silence and black arm bands with flags at half mast – but more an attitude of 'now, come on boys and girls, no crying in the ranks, you've shot a damn sight more of them than they have of you, so take it on the chin and stop trying to play on the public heart strings.'

And if it comes to that, it will not be a good thing for the police or the ordinary public they protect.

Paul Skews may have been a nitwit running free range, who got himself and his young mate killed in fair combat in the eyes of God and man. But police aren't the only ones who leave grieving loved ones behind. Police aren't the only ones with children, wives, brothers, sisters, mothers and fathers. Even Ned Kelly had a mother.

It seems to me that at present when a cop and a crim die, the tears that flow from the eyes of the policeman's mother are the only tears the media and general public focus on.

But things are changing as the death toll mounts. You watch, the police are being pushed into becoming their own worst enemy through no fault of their own.

I HEAR on the news that the police who blew Paul Skews and his young mate away may be called upon to do a full re-enactment of the whole thing. That will be a monumental waste of time.

I recall a conversation I once had with the late Detective-Sergeant John Hill of the Homicide Squad in Melbourne. He believed guilty people who planned to plead 'guilty' didn't need to do re-enactments. But he'd much prefer that the guilty people who planned on pleading 'not guilty' do a full re-enactment.

He went on to say that anyone involved in the premeditated death or the accidental death of another had at best a jumbled recall of events and could only recall what they felt happened, what they believed happened, filling in the blank spots with guess work.

Like the man who killed his wife in the bedroom, yet was convinced he killed her in the kitchen. His mind had wiped out all memory of anything happening in the bedroom.

And the woman who vividly remembers stabbing her husband once and once only, yet he was stabbed 50 times.

The man who recalled firing his gun over and over again, yet only one bullet wound was found. Another man remembered firing one shot when there were six shots in the body.

People can be ready and more than willing to confess to the murder of a family member or loved one or business partner. Yet at the re-enactment they are unable to relive the event correctly in action and have to be prompted by police who had already taken a previous statement.

Re-enactments were a fiasco according to Big John Hill, and in most cases the only reason they did re-enactments was to cover themselves in case the accused changed his mind and pleaded not guilty at court, or to try to get someone who 'claimed' it was an accident to trip himself up.

But even then, death seemed to leave large blank spots on the human brain which made re-enactments a bit of a joke.

Speaking for myself I can back that up. Once the guns come out the blood jumps through the veins at a 1000 miles per hour, the heart and the brain are screaming together. Don't get me wrong. It's a fantastic rush.

I love pulling the trigger, when it's called for. But the rush of it all does leave blank spots on the brain. The same thing seems to happen to the memories of people who witness a shooting, the shock or rush of it all leaves blank spots on the brain. One second seems like ten seconds, ten seconds seems like 60 seconds. Three shots can seem like six.

The rush, shock, fear, nerves – call it what you will – blanks large and important parts of the memory out so you have to fill in the blank spots with what could have happened, or what you felt, or believed happened.

But instead of saying 'shit, that part's a bit of a blur in my memory', they say, 'Yes, Yes, I did this. I stood here. I fired this way' and make it up as they go along, frightened of looking foolish or guilty or whatever and come across looking like lying ratbags.

Yet somehow no-one who has been involved in the murder, or killing, of anyone has ever confessed to anything less than total recall.

What a lot of shit unless they are using the old 'I don't remember a bloody thing defence'. The truth is, at best you can recall 80 to 90 per cent but there will always be parts of it that play havoc with the mind and memory.

That's the way it is. Re-enactments are highly questionable. Some courts seem to love them, lawyers carry on over them as if they are the point of truth. We've all watched too much television. I'd much rather watch *Debbie Does Dallas* than *Julian Does Hoddle Street*. Ha ha.

WHILE on this subject, I read in the newspapers that the former Victorian State Coroner Mr Hal Hallenstein has given the Victoria Police a bit of a bagging over the police shootings, and Father Peter Norden has also been screaming his lungs out.

I've never met Hallenstein and don't wish to meet him. I have sent a few clients to him, but that is another story. I do, however, know Father Norden. He took over as the Pentridge priest from Father Brosnan.

I always found Father Norden to be a classic Left-wing bleeding heart. A nice fellow in himself and very caring and kindly and well-intentioned, but not in touch with the reality of the prison, the criminal world or the men he was dealing with. He is a Roman Catholic Priest, Society of Jesus, Jesuit. I used to have many religious and political debates with him.

The Jesuit order, Society of Jesus was founded by Ignatius Loyola in 1534. He was a Spanish soldier turned priest who acted as an informer and inquisitor for the Spanish inquisition, a small point the modern day Jesuit order don't like to mention. He was an ultra-political animal — a sly, treacherous bastard who climbed over the bodies of a thousand men. He could have been a politician, if he'd had better superannuation, a gold travel pass, and free tickets to a Gold Coast brothel.

Loyola was involved in the death of kings and even popes. Political intrigue and conspiracy has haunted the Society of Jesus ever since and the Jesuit Order certainly does seem to have a great interest in matters social and political.

They are without doubt the most powerful order within the

Catholic Church. I used to joke with Father Norden that the Jesuits were the Vatican mafia and that they should stick to what they know most about.

'What's that,' Father Norden would reply. 'Killing popes and plotting the overthrow of South American dictatorships. Ha ha.'

I think it's fair to say that I wasn't his favorite prisoner in spite of our smiles.

Now, to get back to these bloody police shootings. It's like the monkey who roared like a lion at night and made all the animals in the jungle run away in panic and fear.

The monkey started to think he was a lion because all the animals ran in fear of him at night. It was dark, none of the animals could see that the roaring monster was just a little monkey and so the monkey continued to rant and roar.

Even the elephants ran away with the wolves and jackals, and the monkey roared out 'I am king of the jungle'. Then one night the monkey came across a lion and the monkey roared and growled, but instead of running away in fear the lion charged forward and pounced on the monkey and tore him to shreds.

In the morning all the animals came to look, and when they saw the dead monkey they all cried and asked the lion why he killed the poor monkey. The old lion looked at the dead monkey and, feeling a bit puzzled himself, he said 'he's a dead monkey now, but last night he was a lion'.

I guess the moral is if all you've got is a banana in your hand you'd better eat it and stop waving it about trying to pretend it's a shotgun, and if you're a monkey stay in the trees and don't run around the jungle pretending to be a lion. If anybody wants to roar like lions then they better make sure they have the teeth and claws to back it up. I for one have no tears for dead monkeys. The world is full of real dangers, and police are no different from any other people. When you hear the lion roar you either fill it full of lead, or run like a rat. You certainly do not stop to check to see if it's a real one or you

Above: Tauree Cleaver must learn to hold onto the bars.

Below: Gloria Kermond – my mate Bucky says he wouldn't know whether to plonk her or punch on with her.

Ball bearing

Not Ball bearing

Ball bearing child

'To my darling Mark! Especially for you. Justine XXX'.

It's enough to make you break out in a sweat! (*clockwise from top left*) Justine,
Tashliene, Big Margaret and Gloria.

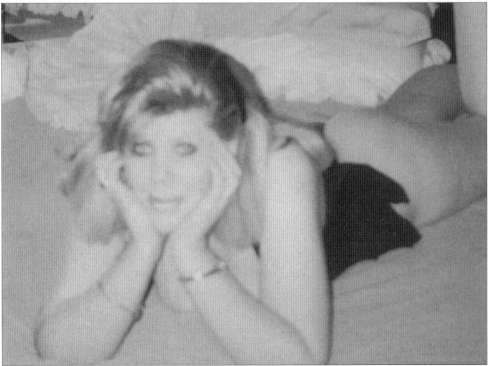

Above left: Rachell McBain.

Above right and below: My fiancée, Mary-Ann Hodge.

Above: Loneliness of the long-distance gunman … the late Tony Tanner (in the dark coat) joins a race at Risdon in 1989. Micky Marlow (wearing long trousers and boots) was rumoured to be the last to see him alive before he disappeared in 1991.

Below: My mad mate Micky Chatters goes for the crunch against the University Boys in the clink.

Above: Big Tony Barron getting his whack.

Below: They tell me these bats can be used to play cricket as well.

Above: Another night out with the Spartan Debating Club.

Below: Rock star Jimmy Barnes asking my former girlfriend Margaret for my autograph. Ha ha.

A waste of a life.

The lovely Melissa … just good friends.

I always knew the Hell's Angels were kings when it came to speed ... so did the cops. These are surveillance pictures of the Greenslopes amphetamine lab near Melbourne.

Above: The late John Paul Madden died in a suspicious road accident and, *below*, Anton Kenny died in a suspicious swimming accident – he was found with no legs. In a 44-gallon drum.

The police move in on the boys at Greenslopes.

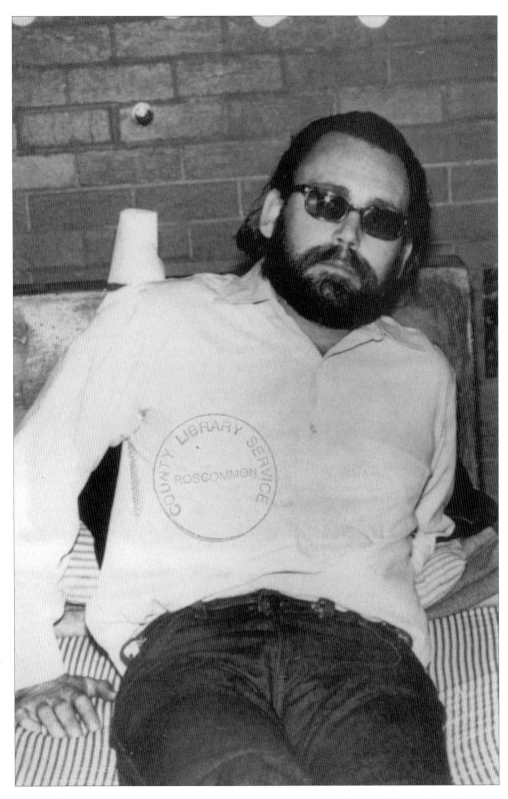

International Hell's Angel trouble 'shooter' James Patton 'Jim Jim' Brandes, following his arrest in Melbourne, hours after stepping off a plane from the U.S.

could end up dead. And I'm no police lover. I'm a lover of self defence and I am a great believer in every human having a God-given right to self defence.

I reckon the jungle is becoming to full of monkeys who roar like lions, and when they die all that anyone sees, in hindsight, is the poor dead monkey and they all blame the poor old lion.

I've shot a few of these roaring monkeys myself. Personally I can't stand the little bastards. Mind you, some of them gave me a few 'gorillas' if I ever put my hand out. And some were more chumps than chimps.

A SMALL topic of comic interest unique to the criminal world inside and outside prison that has always given me much amusement over the years is the way crooks divvy up their ill-gotten gains.

The very best of friends will gather to whack up the booty, and each man will sit at the table with his hand on his gun butt as the pie gets cut up. Very often a six-man gang can meet to whack up the proceeds and turn into a three or four-man gang in a few bloody moments of gunfire.

Half the gang wars in and out of a prison have been sparked by ill will over the unequal division of cash and goods. Squabbles over money are never ending and every weekend at the card tables in every jail yard, this fine criminal tradition is carried on.

It reminds me of another story told to me as a small boy by my dear old Dad, who was a sort of a bent Aussie version of Rudyard Kipling or Aesop.

In relation to the equal division of funds, there is the yarn of the lion, the fox and the donkey who agree to form a partnership and go out hunting. They were the very best of comrades in arms and staunch and solid friends and plundered and killed with scant regard.

At the end of their hunting adventure the lion told the donkey to share the proceeds out. The donkey divided the booty out into three equal parts, making sure to be extra careful and correct that each pile of goodies was exactly the same size and weight.

When he was done the donkey said to the lion, 'you are king of the jungle so you have first pick'. The lion said 'thank you, my dear friend donkey'. Then the lion looked at the three large piles of game, gold and goodies and all manner of good things to eat and he turned and sprang at the donkey in a fury and rage and killed and devoured him.

When the lion had finished licking the donkey's blood from his claws, he looked at the terrified fox and said, 'Dear old foxy, my fine fellow, would you be so good as to share out and divide the proceeds again into two piles. The donkey, bless his heart, won't be needing his.'

The cunning fox then set about collecting all the piles of goodies, gold and game and pushing it into one giant pile leaving only a few small left over tidbits in a very tiny pile for himself. Then the fox said, 'Lion, my dear fellow, please take your pick.'

The lion looked at the tiny pile and then at the large pile and picked the large pile, then turned and said to the fox, 'By the way my dear foxy, who on earth taught you to share things out in such a manner?'

'The donkey,' replied the fox. Ha ha.

My Dad and his yarns. When the old boy wasn't punching my head in for assorted crimes that I may have committed, he was spinning me some fable. These little yarns went a long way in building my tactical and strategic psychology.

He had another yarn I thought was terrific. The old lion was too slow to hunt or fight for his food so he decided to use his wits. He lay down in a cave and pretended to be sick and when any animal came to visit him he ate them.

It's a trick many humans use in various forms. The lion lay in the cave for a long time and animals from all over came to visit their sick king and all were eaten.

The cunning fox came to visit but stood outside the cave and called inside, 'I've come to visit, King Lion. How are you?'

'Oh my dear old fox,' cried the lion, 'how nice of you to visit. What a dear old foxy you are. Please come inside to visit.'

'No,' said the fox, 'it's such a nice day, I think I'll stand out here in the sun.'

'But foxy,' cried the old lion, 'please come in. All the other animals in the jungle have and we had such nice visits.'

The fox, being ever so polite, but not stupid, said, 'Dear lion, I'm sure you did have a nice visit with all of them. The trouble is, my dear old fellow, I can see a lot of tracks going into your cave but no tracks at all coming out.'

My old Dad's yarns taught me a lot. Experience and brains will always beat youth and brawn. I was strong and tough when I was 18, but I was far more dangerous when I was ten years older. I am not as strong as I once was but I am not a man to cross.

A PHILOSOPHER is someone who points out the bleeding obvious to people who are too thick-headed to think of it themselves.

Having said that, allow me to indulge in a little philosophy. Imagine that on the night before Doomsday a candlelit dinner party will be held for the 12 remaining people on the face of the earth who are not members of the public service.

The topic of the most memorable men in the history of the human race will be raised in heated conversation over the last remaining dozen bottles of Grange Hermitage that haven't been sold to the Japanese.

The most memorable men in human history … who will they be? It's a big question.

It's not Doomsday tomorrow and I'm not one of the men seated at that table, but I'm betting London to a brick that in the minds of men a thousand years from now, or whenever, only two sorts of men will be remembered: poets and killers.

We look back and who do we remember in Australia? Lawson, Paterson and Ned Kelly. Look at America, a land littered with legends. Who stands above them all? Mark Twain and Lee Harvey Oswald. Look at Irish history and who do we have? James Joyce and Daniel O'Connell. O'Connell being a humble Irish politician which is the same as a killer, and certainly thought of as a killer by his enemies.

What about the history of England? My bet would be William Shakespeare and Jack the Ripper. In Germany we have Nietzsche and Hitler. In Russia we have Leo Tolstoy and Joe Stalin.

The list goes on and on. The only truly good men history will remember who were not killers or poets will be the prophet Mohammed and Jesus Christ. But neither of them were ordinary men. They had God's hand on their shoulders.

But of the ordinary men who will be remembered – killers and poets keep coming up. It's funny, but a great many of these men were hated or heavily criticised during their lifetime.

The reason in relation to poets is simple. Poets are rarely understood by men of their own generation and are always ahead of their time. Hence the next generation and following generations applaud them.

The answer in relation to killers is just as simple. A murder today is a tragic horror, but a murder yesterday is history and all men have a fascination with history.

And then there is the elite class – killer poets like my good self who can, write, fight, bite, light, smite and, when need be, say goodnight.

While I very much doubt that my name will be raised at the Doomsday dinner party, I suspect that I will be thought of more kindly after my death than while I'm alive. What strange creatures human being are. Ha ha.

Talking of poetry, I was called upon by the Spartan Debating Club recently and I thought I'd give the buggers a bit of the old Banjo Paterson.

On the outer Barcoo where the churches are few,
  And men of religion are scanty,
  On a road never crossed except by folks that are lost,
  One Michael Magee had a shanty ...

WELL, I was no sooner into my first verse then the ignorant bastards started booing me down. It's a sad day indeed when the immortal Banjo is mocked and booed, because it wasn't me they were booing, it was the great Banjo. As an Aussie it was a sad thing to see.

These bums would think a poet laureate is an endangered species of native parrot.

I remember on Friday and Saturday nights at the Station Hotel in Greville Street, Prahran, they would have live rock bands playing back in the early 70s. Me and Cowboy Johnny, Dave the Jew, Terry the Tank, Solly the Jew and now and again Piss Ant Normie, or Robert Lochrie and once or twice even old Horatio Morris would pop in to see me.

Vincent Villeroy used to catch my act for a giggle but in general it was just me and the Surrey Road crew.

When the rock band was having its break I would grab the microphone and with it in one hand and a jug of beer in the other I would entertain the drunken crowd with a recital of Banjo Paterson's poems.

When we got to *The Man from Ironbark,* the whole pub would stand in silent reverence while I recited. When I'd finished the crowd went mad and clapped and cheered like crazy. I'm sorry to say that the days of me knowing Banjo Paterson poems off by heart are over. I've forgotten the ones I knew, all except for *The Man From Ironbark*.

Of course, the people in the pub remained respectfully silent while I gave the recital. I now look back on it all and wonder if it was due to me being a latter day Leonard Teale or because the Cowboy and the Jew were both armed and crazy and big fans of Paterson. To talk during *Ironbark* was not a healthy thing to do.

IT'S sad for me to see the way poor old Aussieland is going. As I've said before, I call it the Americanisation of Australia, which is fast becoming a shadow of its former self.

I'm not talking about the land the politicians see because the only glimpse of Australia they get is out the limo window on the drive from Parliament House to the TV studio.

I'm talking about the real Australia. The faces in the street. The ordinary battler's culture has been sold to the bloody Yanks and the land he walks on has been sold to the Japs.

The Americans have even done it to our sport. What's every bugger playing these days? Bloody basketball. When I grew up basketball was a girl's game; boys played footy or cricket.

Yes, let's all play bloody basketball, spit on Banjo Paterson and all become Yankee Doodle puppets.

Even the criminal world has all gone American or South American. And the police are all being trained in classic American tactics and strategies. Our schools and prisons have all gone American. The whole thing makes me spew. Australia has adopted every bad idea that has ever come out of Yankee land.

Between the Yanks and the Japs they have completely rooted us. We'll be eating raw fish with a side order of fries, next. And if that doesn't make you sick, nothing will.

CHAPTER 28

FRANKIE GETS CAUGHT SPEEDING AND OTHER TALES

MY old mate Frankie Waghorn could spin a yarn, and there was none better than his brief experimentation with the drug speed, otherwise known as methamphetamine.

Frankie went to a party and was offered some speed and swallowed a full gram down with a can of lemonade. He then went home to his mother's place in West Heidelberg and thought that it would be a good idea to vacuum the house, seeing that his mother was away.

So Frankie proceeded to clean the house at 3am. When he had finished he thought it would be a good idea to vacuum the driveway, so he got an extension cord and started vacuuming the driveway.

When he finished, he noticed that the footpath was a bit dirty and ran inside and came back out with a second extension cord and gave the footpath in front of his house a good going over.

The neighbours rang the police, as the vacuum cleaner was kicking up a terrible racket. When the police arrived they found Frankie and the overworked Hoover in the middle of Waterdale Road in front of his mother's house.

There was no criminal offence involved, although they did breathalyse my poor old mate. The mind boggles at what the charge would have been had he been drunk!

Most short bar room yarns, while being comic and true, tend to be of a sexual nature. I'm led to believe Henry Lawson had a vast collection of dirty yarns he told in pubs but never wrote down, and even the great Banjo Paterson had a few slightly blue ditties up his sleeve.

But I'm afraid my dirty ditties and short stories are somewhat bluer that anything the gentle Banjo ever told.

Micky Marlow and the lady with the club foot is a favorite. However, good taste begs that I spare you the sordid details of that particular yarn. A recent yarn I picked up a short while ago involved Bucky and the blind girl, which puts the tale of Micky Marlow and the chick with the club foot in the shade.

Comic story telling and joke telling and the telling of wild bar room yarns was once a classic Aussie past time, sadly fading in the pubs, clubs, racetracks and prisons. But the art is not dead yet. There was a time when every Aussie had at least one wild yarn up his sleeve and I'm one Aussie with a sleeve full of the bastards. Ha ha. My mate Pat Burling together with my old friend Andy Hutton had a rip roaring New Year's eve at the Retreat Hotel on Invermay Road at the bottom of Mowbray Hill in Launceston.

Pat is a bit of a mad bugger with a few drinks in him. At six foot and 100 kilos he fights like a threshing machine. Pat and Andy were having a quiet drink in the bar of the Retreat and Pat said to Andy, 'as soon as we finish these drinks you smash that bloke over there and I'll smash this one here'. And Andy, not quite understanding the plan, said 'Right' and put his drink down and walked across the bar room and proceeded to swing punches.

The pub broke out in total chaos and Pat jumped in swinging punches at a 100 miles per hour. Andy Hutton has the courage of a lion but isn't the world's best punch-on artist and was getting punched to the floor.

He kept getting back up swinging his fists and was promptly punched back to the deck but refused to give in. Meanwhile Big Pat was taking on all comers in grand fashion, but it all got too much.

He tossed the car keys to Andy and yelled 'Get the gun.' Andy grabbed the keys, ran outside and grabbed the gun. Andy was a former member of my old crew, the hole in the head shooting club, and drunk in charge of a firearm he is a bloody menace, believe me.

Anyway, he proceeded to blast the shit out of the pub, with men ducking for cover and diving to the ground all over the place.

Big Pat Burling made good his escape and they both jumped in their car and took off up Mowbray Hill with a line of police cars on their tail. Pat hung the gun out the window and aimed it at the police cars behind him and yelled 'Get a bit of this into ya – you bastards' and bang, bang, bang. Then the bloody gun jammed. Needless to say both Pat and Andy got themselves pinched and Pat accidentally lost the sight in his right eye after the following interview got a bit out of hand.

As we all know, there is no such thing as police violence so perish the thought that poor Pat was the victim of foul play in the police station. Andy, who has a plate in his skull, needed to see a panel beater after the police interview to get the plate straightened out. Ha ha.

Naturally enough, the police get a bit funny after they have been shot at and tend to suffer mood swings. The bloody Retreat Hotel is known locally as the little police station at the bottom of the hill as you only have to fart and the police get called and they really get pissed off if you pull a gun out. My favorite pub in Invermay, which is like the little Footscray of Launceston, is the Inveresk Hotel in Dry Street, Invermay. You could fire a cannon in the bar of the Inveresk and everyone would mind their own business, provided you didn't hit the TV set.

What Pat and Andy were doing in the Retreat is a puzzle. Anyway, mad Andy Hutton, my old comrade-in-arms, is out and about, a free man. With good lawyers and a lot of luck anything can happen. Pat Burling is in here with me. Poor bugger, he looks a bit funny with his pirate eye patch on.

The strange thing is that Pat's cousin, Big Josh Burling, is also blind in one eye. Pat, nicknamed 'Mumbles', is one of the funniest men you'd ever come across, and a better fellow you'd never meet in a day's march. While I'm sorry to see him in jail again the prison would be a much duller place without him. Having a few good blokes around you makes all the difference.

CHAPTER 29

HOW THE ANGELS ALMOST ROLLED THE BALL

SOME of the so-called outlaw motorcycle gangs have been identified by Australian law enforcement agencies as prime examples of sophisticated organised crime groups.

Police, through Operation Wing Clipping, identified the Hell's Angels as a major influence in the production and distribution of amphetamines in the 1980s.

In 1982 a police task force, Omega Two, found a Hell's Angels amphetamines factory in Wattle Glen, known as Greenslopes.

The factory was potentially capable of producing 22.5 kilos of high quality amphetamines a week. Four trials and five years later, four of the Angels were found guilty of producing amphetamines.

At one point a US Hell's Angel hitman, James Paton Brandes, arrived in Melbourne, but was apprehended after police were told that he had arrived to kill one of the Omega team.

According to an FBI report on outlaw motorcycle gangs, 'The Hell's Angels Motorcycle gang has become a highly professional, sophisticated organisation involved in criminal activities including the acquisition and

*infiltration of legitimate businesses to launder the immense profits gained
from illicit drug dealings.'*

SOMEHOW I got myself involved in motorcycle club politics when
I became friendly with various characters in Tassie, and I have paid
the price.

However, it wasn't the first time. That is one of my big problems.
I don't seem to learn from my mistakes. Many years ago, the man
who could have run the Melbourne underworld before he lost
interest, Mad Charlie, ended up connected with the Melbourne
chapter of the Hell's Angels Motorcycle Club.

It is a matter which embarrassed the rough, tough bikers no end.
According to rumor it involved the kidnapping of the Hell's Angels
speed amphetamine cook and the bashing of two high-ranking Hell's
Angels outside a Melbourne nightclub.

The affair is, of course, only rumor, and the Angels would, no
doubt deny it. Certainly no action was ever taken against Mad
Charlie. The fact that Charlie could probably muster a dozen of
Melbourne's most noted nut cases with more guns than God at a
moment's notice, may have had something to do with it.

I had a small falling out with an Italian heroin dealer named Tony
Zampaglione, a would-be mafia type. He got around A Division of
Pentridge with his brother Sam and a Hell's Angels bodyguard
named 'Jock'.

I had to give Tony a foot up the backside on a matter of prison
protocol and the Hell's Angel handed in his resignation about ten
seconds later. Meanwhile, I was maintaining close contact with one
of the most powerful Hell's Angels in the country, a man I call the
'Lawyer', and various other members of the club who had
considerable influence on a national level.

Yet my disregard of Zampaglione and his friendship with various
members of the Melbourne chapter of the Angels, and my friendship
with Mad Charlie, who, according to rumor, had embarrassed the

Melbourne chapter greatly, forced me unwillingly into the shadowy world of biker politics.

In 1987 I had arranged with my own contacts in the Hell's Angels to back them in an internal blood war that seemed likely to happen. It was all to do with a power struggle within the club. The war never took place and my help was never needed. But it became known that I was the ace in the hole for one side in a bikie war.

However, for this and other reasons my name is not popular in the ranks of the Melbourne Chapter of the Angels. To add insult to bloody injury, Mad Charlie introduced me to a beautiful big-bosomed blonde glamor girl named Melissa.

Melissa and myself became great and good friends and are still friendly to this day. However, in 1987 Melissa was also the much loved and jealously guarded girlfriend of 'Ballbearing', the President of the Melbourne chapter of the Angels.

'Ballbearing' was part of the internal power struggle that involved my old friend and comrade 'the Lawyer', so the plot thickened. The set-up is the way the game is played and I must admit that I always feared a set-up from the Angels, as they had the cold cash power and connections to set any one up in those days. However, old friends high up in the Angels told me not to worry.

The Hell's Angels, unlike other bike clubs, are businessmen. It may not be the Melbourne Club but it is just about as powerful and a lot more harmful to your health. The Angels is no longer a bike club, it is a multi-national conglomerate. They are not petty people and they know mindless wars are bad for business. Self defence they will agree to, but no-one was going to bother trying to kill me because I was close, in a platonic way, naturally, to the President's girl.

Melissa is no longer with 'Ballbearing' and lives happily a long way from Melbourne by the beach in the sun. But the spider's web of shadows involved in biker politics is mind numbing and still hangs over me. But I am close to figuring out the spider's web in relation to myself and certain people. Or certain person.

WHO shot the idiot who got me into this mess and why is no longer a mystery to me, but to understand why he gave Crown evidence against me and tossed my name into the ring I must explain biker politics.

First, you have to know that the backbone of all the main players in the biker gangs of this country and overseas is drugs.

Overseas it's cocaine and meth amphetamine. However, in Australia it is 100% meth amphetamine. The bike gangs introduced it to Australia and to this day control its manufacture. The Angels are at the top of the bike world in Australia. The Angels membership is small and elite. It is not the largest club in Australia, but by far the richest and the most powerful.

There are two sorts of biker clubs: those affiliated with the Angels and those which are not. The club with the closest affiliation with the Angels is the Coffin Cheaters. Then there is the Outlaws, an American club with power in America that runs close and in some ways rivals the Hell's Angels, but in Australia it is not a large club.

The Outlaws have mainland chapters in Victoria and are growing fast, and have no affiliation with the Angels. The Outlaws, do, however have an affiliation with the Black Uhlans MC, a large and powerful mainland club. The idiot I mentioned above fell out with the Outlaws and was no longer their president and when I was getting around with him his best friend and right hand man was Black Uhlans Larry, a former president of the NSW chapter of the Black Uhlans.

Yet while the idiot had fallen out with the Tasmanian chapter of the Outlaws, he maintained a close friendship with 'Doughnut', a member of the Victorian chapter of the Outlaws.

Now the Outlaws and the Hell's Angels had no affiliation whatsoever, in fact in some quarters there was almost a warlike feeling between the two. Interestingly, the bloke I'm talking about was most welcome at the Satan's Riders club house in Launceston. And yet the Satan's Riders and the Outlaws were not very friendly and, unlike the Outlaws, the Satan's Riders had a loose affiliation with the Hell's Angels.

I found the fact that this bloke got on well with a club that was affiliated with the Angels most odd, as the Black Uhlans, his protectors, had no affiliation with the Angels.

The same matter was raised at my trial. There is no way in the world, in my opinion, that he would have given Crown evidence against anyone, let alone false Crown evidence without the silent approval of one of the bike gangs. Even though he has broken the code by giving evidence it appears he is still accepted for some strange reason by some biker clubs in Tassie who should know better. Wouldn't it be funny if, in time to come, I was to find out that this particular person gave evidence against me just because I was suspected of getting on too well with the wrong girl in 1987? It wouldn't be the first time a seemingly harmless friendship led to serious consequences.

Fact is most certainly stranger than fiction. Food for thought.

Forgive me for rambling on about this, but the mystery of why the fool gave evidence against me will haunt me until I solve the puzzle. To do what he did would mean that he would have to have the blessing of at least one bike club. I am not a member of any bike club, but during my years in Pentridge I befriended some powerful members of powerful bike gangs.

I have contacts in the biker world from Australia to Oakland, California, simple friendships that I have maintained. These friendships allow me a certain insight, but no one man will ever know all about the interconnected, almost incestuous, love-hate friendships and rivalries that exist within the motorcycle gang world.

If you add drugs and money to the spider's web of biker politics you have total insanity. I tumbled my way into this maze without really meaning to do so and if I ever get out of this jail I have no intention of tumbling into it again.

To give you another example of the spider web: There I am in

1987 meeting with one of the most powerful members of the Hell's Angels in Australia, being consulted in relation to the internal power struggle in the Victorian chapter. The idea was to contract work out to outsiders to solve internal problems. Meaning that some Hell's Angels were arranging to have other Hell's Angels killed because they themselves couldn't kill their own brothers within the club and still maintain their positions, respect and authority. It was a political power struggle to gain financial control. And it was resolved without bloodshed and I and others were never called upon as previously agreed.

Meanwhile, as I mentioned, I was seeing the girlfriend of the President of the Melbourne chapter.

Later, in Tasmania in 1992, Cracker Phillips and myself and the nitwit were invited to drink at the fortress-like club house of the Satan's Riders in Launceston.

The Satan's Riders did not get along with the Outlaws, who in turn didn't get along to well with the Hobart based Devil's Henchmen club either.

The Devil's Henchmen didn't get along to well with Black Uhlans Larry, righthand man to the other bloke I was with. Yet once inside the Satan's Riders club house, there was he was with members of the Satan's Riders MC and a member of the Devil's Henchmen all in secret conversation – while Cracker Phillips and my good self drank with other members of the club trying to pinpoint just who was on whose side and who was really loyal to who. It was a nightmare as these people play the smiling face politics, a game I know a great deal about.

However, in the biker world many men within many clubs are all playing the smiling treachery game and in the end, in spite of my contacts in this scene, I am a fish out of water. The bike gangs avoid blood wars and feuds with members of the mainstream underworld for the same reason – they are fish out of water. And the mainstream criminal world tries to avoid blood feuds with the biker world.

The drugs and money join the two together, but neither side trusts the other totally as they are of two different worlds. So for me to ever find out the truth about the whole shooting fiasco is probably something I will never do, and in the end I only have myself to blame.

I BEG to make a small postscript to my previous remarks in relation to that stalwart body of men, the Hell's Angels Motorcycle Club, and their on-again, off-again president, Mr Christopher Gerald Coelho, alias 'Ballbearing'. I think I should make it perfectly clear once more that I was in no way involved in any conspiracy to murder the good Mr Coelho, or anyone else connected with the Hell's Angels.

Perish the thought. The people I was dealing with were trying to do everything in their power to avoid having to kill any member of their own club. I simply agreed to lend a helping hand should a helping hand be required. 'The Lawyer' and his cohorts spoke in riddles and I suspect they were partaking of speed, and were a touch paranoid. They believed that there was a small handful of club members, Ballbearing being one, that might have needed sorting out. The Lawyer and his brothers in plots and plans were doing everything in their power to avoid trouble and pull the club together.

So it was in fact a conspiracy not to murder. Talking to the Hell's Angels is akin to talking to the KGB. I was asked to be at the ready to hit and hit hard. They wanted an attack from outside the club so as to even scores, and at the same time pull the whole club together against a common enemy.

The theory was that any action I might take would be blamed on others, such as another motorcycle club involved in the methamphetamine industry. It was very involved.

There I was in the back of a hire car limousine with a Hell's Angel wearing a three-piece suit and two others in leathers and full colors wearing their patches, snorting speed as the limo drove around and around St Kilda.

Two of them were off their faces at a thousand miles per hour. I was half pissed as always and The Lawyer was brilliant, but semi-mad.

I got the impression that in order to call a halt to the civil war that was raging within the club, the thinking was that if one, two or three of its members were killed – such as, for instance, Ballbearing, Vinnie and Jaw – and their deaths were blamed on another club, it would end all internal hostilities and pull the club together.

The problem was knowing which way Ray Hamment would jump, as he was very close to Bearing and not a total fool and a powerful and respected member of the club. And he was in prison at the time, which was a problem.

Ray could be fixed from behind prison walls, but that would prove professional criminal or mainstream underworld involvement and not another club. It was all very KGB.

It went from plots to kill to plans for peace. Phone calls to America, the whole box and dice, all mixed with heads full of speed. I was starting to wonder why I'd even been called in, unless it was to kill me after I'd killed others.

I agreed to help if needed – in the name of old friendship – yet agreed on nothing specific. It was more thinking out loud using me as a strategic and tactical sounding board. Then it all vanished.

The message was: 'She's sweet, Chopper. We'll handle it'. And that was that. I agreed to kill no-one. I'd like to make that perfectly clear. As I said before, the politics of the motorcycle gang world is a spider's web of shadows. The buggers have more twists and turns than the Freemasons. Ha ha ha.

I TURNED 39 on the 17th of November, 1993, in the remand yard at Risdon Prison. Meanwhile on the same day at the Hobart Supreme Court the nephew of my old mate – and now bitter enemy, referred to above – was appearing on a charge of perverting justice.

Big Mick is a six foot five tall, 20-stone giant who, in my opinion, couldn't be killed or buried without the aid of a fireman's axe and an earth mover. Yet here he was in court pleading not guilty before Mr Justice Slicer and a jury of 12 honest and true Tasmanians, whimpering like an old moll and crying that if he was sent to prison Chopper Read would kill him and that the dreaded Chopper Read had shot his dear uncle and was now after family members. The hillbillies here love the idea of a family feud.

He went on to say that two hit men had come down from the mainland to get his uncle on my orders, but that uncle was being hidden by the police and that the unnamed hit men were now on the hunt for other family members. Sounds like a bloody Peter Corris plot.

Big Mick said he feared for his own life and the lives of his three children. He said if he went to prison Chopper Read would kill him or have him killed and there was further rambling to the effect that I had also killed his brother.

This fiasco all started allegedly on October 22, 1992, when big Mick allegedly went to the home of Hobart lawyer Mr Brian Morgan and in an attempt to have certain charges dropped, dropped heavy hints that Morgan would be well-advised to play ball with him.

Mick's story was that he only went to see Brian Morgan to offer his sad tale re the dreaded Chopper Read, blah blah blah.

So who really cares? Just another nonsense court case with a general steady flow of non-stop rubbish being offered to the judge and jury by all concerned, with Mick's lawyer Mr David Gunson bringing tears to a glass eye, with the 'please feel sorry for my poor client' routine and laying it on with a trowel. Mick was found guilty and remanded in custody to await sentencing and while in the remand yard offered me his profuse apologies for using my name in such a manner.

What the court had not been told was that big Mick had already been in the remand yard with me on a previous occasion and that I had nothing against him whatsoever. In fact, we sat at the same table in the mess room when having our meals. Mick was a giant but I considered him harmless and the sins of his uncle couldn't be blamed

on him or any member of the family and I had told him so. Big Mick
went back to court and walked free with his honor, Mr Justice Slicer,
not imposing a jail sentence proving yet again that if you mention the
name Chopper Read in a Tasmanian court you're on a winner. When
in doubt just blame it on The Chopper.

It would have been simple enough task to check out the tale but
when my name is mentioned in a Tassie court who needs to check
out the facts?

Perish the thought, I can only wonder how many other nephews,
cousins, brothers, relatives of the idiot I'm supposed to have shot
intend to pull this stunt. Heaven knows it works. Good luck to
them all.

The man himself used my name to great effect so why not the rest
of his family. After all, if your horse has been pinched you'd be a fool
not to blame Ned Kelly.

What gets me is that there was some mindless waffle heard in
court to the effect that I'd killed Mick's brother. One would imagine
that this would be cause for some sort of investigation, but no, it
seems that as long as my name is tossed into the cooking pot then
total rubbish can be cooked up, served and eaten with relish in a
Tasmanian Court of law, or police station for that matter.

Oh well, it's not the first time it's happened, and I doubt it will be
the last.

CHAPTER 30

FICKLE FRIENDSHIPS

FRIENDSHIP is a funny thing. When the good times roll everyone wants to rock and roll with you and when the shit hits the fan you're on your own. Except, in my case, for a small stalwart group of people who have stood with me in my time of trouble.

My first lesson in this was when I was just a little kid going to Mornington State School in grade three. There was me, Garry Oliver, Kevin Sweeny, Rodger Gully, Peter Burrows, Billy East and Graeme Starr.

We were a jolly old band of scallywag boyhood mates. Behind the school on a walk to the beach we would cut through behind a row of old houses.

Old man Ferguson kept a dozen or so large apple trees in his backyard, all of which hung heavy with beautiful apples. It was a temptation to any group of boys, but old pop Ferguson kept a shotgun and was a gruff and grumpy old bastard. His backyard had no fence but was protected by a large very prickly row of Hawthorn bushes, with long hard spiky thorns.

There was only one way into Pop Ferguson's yard and that was a small hole we could all crawl through, single file. It was slow and careful going, so as not to get pricked.

Once in the yard we were all loyal and true comrades in arms. But as we picked the apples old Pop Ferguson came out onto his back porch with his shotgun and punched a shot into the air and yelled: 'piss off you young bastards, I'll skin the bloody lot of you', and we took off at a 100 miles per hour.

On the way in we were seven small boys all the very best of friends, one for all and all for one, but running for our lives and with old man Ferguson on our tail with his shotgun, we were suddenly all pushing each other out of the way to get through the one small hole in the Hawthorn bush.

The one for all and all for one brotherhood had turned into a screaming panic-stricken rabble of every boy for himself. One of life's small lessons learnt early.

Graeme Starr was the leader of our gang of grade three bandits, and Pop Ferguson's apple trees were a constant source of temptation in spite of the shotgun.

We must have stabbed ourselves a hundred times over on the thorns, making good our escape after apple raids. Then the old man set rabbit traps and put them in the hole in the Hawthorn bush, as well as the backyard.

In the end it was all too much, and then we realised that the lady in the house at the end of the road kept grapefruit trees. They weren't as nice as Pop Ferguson's apples, but a damn sight safer to pinch.

So we have two lessons learnt. All the security in the world won't stop crime – it just moves it onto another location. And the most important lesson of all when the shit hits the fan the best of mates will scramble over each other to get through the escape hatch.

None of us can deny the spirit of Gallipoli and the bravery of the Anzacs and all, but in reality when the shit hits the fan the Aussie anthem is 'Every man for himself'. What they call the Dingo Principle.

THIS is a short postscript in relation to Harry the Greek. I shouldn't laugh but how's this for black comedy. After four years in jail down here in Tassie he got out recently. He was highly excited and was worrying about what clothes he would wear and what he would do first.

He was all set to go and live with his mate Jimmy, who runs a pub in a small town over here. A party was planned and Jimmy had driven down to pick him up. As it was winter and Harry didn't have any warm clothes I gave him a leather jacket.

He came down to the jail laundry and had his last shower and got dressed and shook hands with all the boys including Eddy the head, the boss of the laundry. He said goodbye to all the screws. It was quite a sad moment watching him get all set to leave.

It only served to remind me that I was remaining behind. Anyway, Harry got all dressed up, put on his imitation made-in-Hong Kong Rolex wrist watch and waved us all goodbye … and then had the handcuffs slapped on him by three detectives and got extradited back to Melbourne over an old armed robbery.

Poor old Harry's arse caved in. His mate Jimmy was out the front of the prison waiting to drive Harry home to the pub, but the police drove him to court and then to the airport. He didn't even get to fly business class.

I can't recall feeling sorry for many people, but I felt sorry for Harry. How's that, four years jail, convinced you're getting out and bang – you're in Pentridge. It's enough to bring a tear to a glass eye.

MY old mate Robert Lochrie and his third wife Jenny have left Victoria to retire to Surfers Paradise. There was a bit of trouble in Victoria concerning Loxy and a traffic accident with two members of a well known motorcycle club. Both bikies were injured, but you will be relieved to know that the Fairlane Loxy was driving was not damaged.

On the way to Surfers, Loxy landed up in Bathurst Jail for a month over some punch up, but he and his good lady wife are now both happily living in the sunshine. His third bloody wife. I don't know how the pineapple-headed bastard does it. He's got a face like five miles of bad road, but pulls more pussy than a Chinese restaurant.

There are only a few blokes from my teenage years still alive and kicking and Loxy is one of them. He has suffered probably more physical injuries than I have, and he's still going.

There he is in Surfers Paradise, with a cold can in one hand and a hot chick in the other.

Meanwhile, I'm sitting in an icebox writing this, watching my breath floating around the cell. If I may quote my little mate 'Bucky' yet again ... it's in winter that we really receive the full benefit of our sentence. Ha ha.

CHAPTER 31

THE GAY DEBATE

THE homosexual debate in Tassie is beginning to take on comic proportions. Every time I turn on the radio or television or look at a local newspaper I'm either hearing about, or reading about the homosexual debate with the Tasmanian Attorney General, Mr Ron Cornish, screaming no, no, no! – and in one case using the Bible to back him up – and the United Nations and the Federal Attorney General yelling yes, yes, yes!

I remember many years ago in Pentridge homosexuality had been legalised for a while but no self-confessed homosexual had tried to join the prison service, until this one particular gentleman did and was proud to tell one and all that he was 'as camp as a row of tents'.

They all knocked him back but legal action was threatened and I believe various Government agencies lost their nerve. The gentleman in question got the job and became the queen of comedy overnight.

He was quite clearly homosexual with the limp wrist and the wiggling walk and the lady-like lisping talk. He would mince about the maximum security division, Jika Jika, like the gay musketeer singing old Shirley Bassey numbers. 'The minute you walked in the joint I could see you were a man of distinction a real big spender, Hey big spender, Hey big spender, spend a little time with me.' Ha Ha Ha.

This crap would go on all day long and the little faggot would really rev up the 'Queen of the May' act to get everybody as mad as he could. If they tried to sack him he'd sue their pants off, no pun intended.

Every Christmas, or so he told us, he would holiday in America and after his first year with the prison service returned with a large metal medallion hanging from his key chain that simply read 'I left my heart in San Fransisco.'

But it got beyond a joke, and a few prisoners and prison officers whispered in his ear to straighten himself up and act normal or the staff would turn a blind eye while the inmates kicked a new arsehole into him. He did indeed straighten himself up and went from a bad imitation of Bette Davis to a bad imitation of Humphrey Bogart. And instead of mincing about the jail like Grace Kelly he started marching about the jail like the little drummer boy and acting as butch as he could.

Instead of singing old Shirley Bassey numbers, he started singing American military songs: 'Silver wings upon our chest, we are men, American's best, flying high to save the day where the men of the green beret.' Ha ha.

It was like a cross between John Wayne and Liberace.

He never lost his slightly gay manner but the jail soon knocked him into shape and he became just another screw and the novelty of the gay prison officer was soon forgotten. He was still working in the prison system in 1991 when I last saw him. In fact, he is not a bad bloke at all and proved himself a bloody good prison officer – honest, reliable and good in a trouble situation. He ended up becoming liked by his fellow officers and the inmates, and the comedy that surrounded his early days at the prison was soon forgotten. He still gets the odd bit of trouble over it now and again, but poof or no poof, he turned out to be not a bad fellow at all.

CHAPTER 32

CHOOK KILLING AND CHILD PSYCHOLOGY

OF late I have been gripped with a fear that my old Dad will die while I am in jail, hence the sentimental memories. It is very hard for me to recall any past adventures with my old Dad that are not an out and out comedy.

When I was a little kid growing up we always kept chooks in the backyard, like every second household in the street in Thomastown did. Chooks and homing pigeons were the big go, then. Thomastown back in the 60s was a working class suburb which still had a bit of a rural feel to it.

Every now and again my mother would decide to have roast chook for Sunday dinner – or her version of it, anyway – and my Dad would instruct me to catch one of the chooks. This entailed a race around the backyard for 20 minutes with me running for my life after a squawking flapping fowl, with my Dad sitting on the back steps yelling encouragement to me.

'Go on son you have got him cornered. Take a running dive for him, boy.' It was like the coyote and Road Runner whenever I got near the chook … 'beep beep' and off it went.

Naturally, my Dad thought this was the height of good humor. In the end I would catch the panic-stricken poultry and carry it over to Dad. He would take it and over we would got to the wood pile, where the chopping block was, and Dad would grab the tomahawk.

I would squeal with delight. 'Can I kill him Dad? Please? Go on, can I kill him please?'

'Okay son. I'll hold him and you chop his head off.' And Dad would hold the chook down on the chopping block and I would heft up the tomahawk and Dad would say, 'across the neck, son, a good clean swing. Go on, and don't hit me with the axe.'

I would swing down hard and 'whop', off came the chook's head and Dad would hold the flapping, headless fowl upright and put him on the ground for the final show, the best part of all.

The chook would take off at a flat rate and run around the yard with blood spurting out of its neck. This was sheer magic to me. A headless chook with blood spurting out of its neck running flat out was one of the highlights of my childhood years. It would hit the fence and fall over and somehow get to its feet and take off again. This could go on for a full minute or two, and I was always disappointed to see the chook at last fall over and give up the ghost.

But I can tell you something, those chooks had more dash than a few drug dealers I know. Most of them would keel over as soon as you showed them the axe. Ha, ha.

Watching a chook with no head doing the four minute mile was one thing, but after the show came the hard work. Dad would get a bucket of boiling water and toss the headless chook into the bucket and we would both sit and talk of magic things, like the time Dad reckoned he killed a Japanese soldier by making him eat a plate of my Mother's roast chicken.

I would look at him and say 'are you telling me the truth Dad?'

'No son, but shut up and listen when ya old man's talking.'

'Yes Dad.'

Dad would delight me with such nonsense until the chook in the bucket of boiling water was ready, then the very worst job came. I had to sit on the back steps with the chook in the bucket between my legs and pluck the feathers out.

It was a horrible job, but I would pluck away with my Dad watching my every move. After it was plucked Mum would take it and cook it. 'We should have killed a few more,' I would always say. I thought one would never be enough. That is, until I tasted it. The magnificent roast chicken with all the trimmings that I imagined always ended up being boiled and turned into a chook stew.

After lunch while Mum and my sister, Debbie, washed the dishes Dad would take me up the shop for an icecream and say to me, 'a bit of icecream will get the taste of that poor bloody chook out of our mouths, son. There is no doubt about your mother; she works magic with the pots and pans.'

I knew the answer to that one. 'Yeah,' I'd say, 'black magic, hey Dad?' And Dad would clip me over the head and tell me not to speak ill of my mother's efforts at cooking. But he didn't clip me very hard.

I never liked eating the chooks, but killing the buggers was wonderful fun and one of the great joys of my childhood days. Ah, my old Dad. I love him.

Kids today are bloody spoilt in my opinion. I've been watching a TV documentary on the kids of today and how tough it is for them at school. As far as book learning is concerned I fully agree, but in my day corporal punishment was in vogue and they were tough days, believe me. Half the teachers we had then would be certified if they were still about. I think I started school in 1959 or 1960, and on the first day I got six across the backs of my legs as a little welcome aboard message.

The little kids and all the girls got the cuts across the backs of their legs. The older boys got it across the hands. All the boys loved to watch the girls get the strap across the backs of their legs.

I realise now that some teachers were sadists, and strapping the girls was a great favorite of one teacher. I remember at least once a day he would pull the school fat girl, Bung Hole Judy, out for eating something in class and flog her soundly with a long wooden ruler across the back of her chubby legs.

She wasn't a bad chick, the old Bung Hole. Once, she copped the cuts across the backs of the legs for three days running in front of the whole school at morning assembly, all because she would not tell who broke the headmaster's window. And you don't have to be told, it was me and another kid called Scrapper Scully who broke the window in a rock tossing contest.

Bung Hole Judy had the bad luck to be standing there working her way through a bag of chips and watching us toss yonnies at the headmaster's window. Both our stones hit the window at the same time and me and Scrapper ran like hell, leaving Bung Hole Judy standing, still chewing. The headmaster looked out the window and there was poor Judy looking guilty. 'Did you see who did that?' he yelled.

'Yes' said Judy.

'Who was it?' asked the headmaster.

'I can't tell' said Judy. She stuck rock solid for three days until I owned up and stepped out in assembly on the fourth day. I got six of the best on each hand every day for a week in front of the whole school and won the fair heart of every fat girl in the district for my heroic conduct.

Old Bung Hole had more courage and dash than most crims I know. She would not give me up, which is more than can be said for most so-called gangsters, who start to cry and blubber whenever they get near a police station.

I wonder whatever happened to Judy. She's probably a stunner now. Mornington State School, a great place. If you're out there, Judy, let me know.

At Thomastown State School in grade two I was given six of the best on each hand and made to stand under the school flagpole for an hour in the rain because I did not know the name of Smokey Dawson's horse.

On another occasion at a school in Preston, standing up in front of the class in a spelling contest, I was unable to spell the name of Chips Rafferty and was made to stand under the school bell for the remainder of the day in the middle of winter and given the strap on each hand before let-out, so as to warm my hands, according to the teacher. How thoughtful of him.

These days it is all rap dancing and basketball. Shit, the only people to play basketball in the 60s were poofs and school girls. Boys played footy and cricket. Cricket, the game that made the British Empire great and helped to civilise half the bloody world. Speaking of which, I was flogged silly at Lalor High School for telling a sports master that he could jam his Don Bradman special edition, personally signed cricket bat straight up his clacker. Personally, I think he may have done such things in the privacy of his own bedroom anyway, so I don't know why he was so outraged by my suggestion. But he was. My hands were blue from the bruising of the six of the best on each hand for a week over that lot.

We had to wear full uniforms and do the old 'yes sir, no sir, three bags full sir' routine or we paid for it with our blood, so to speak. These days it's all Reebok runners, back to front baseball caps, and rap dancing at lunch time.

The only sport played now is basketball and spot-the-Aussie. At least we were carefree in my day with the classic Aussie couldn't give a shit attitude. It may have been physically harder but I think it was a bit more relaxed. Today's kids are all yuppie computerised nervous wrecks with drug habits, and a poor sad lot they are too.

WELL, I've just finished spit polishing my Blundstone lace-up boots to a truly mirror shine. I used to spit-polish my old Dad's army boots when I was a little boy. I'd melt the black Nugget by holding a match under the tin with a small amount of Nugget in it, then dip my polishing rag into the melted Nugget and apply it liberally to the boot. Then I'd polish away. When the boots shone I'd then spit on them and go over them with a dry towel.

As I've mentioned, my old Dad was a very violent man toward me as a kid but I loved him, and as I grew older I decided to remember only the good in him and try to forget about the violence as much as possible. He was very loving and kind toward me a lot of the time, and I guess he was no more violent toward me than other fathers of that day and age. I remember once after I didn't polish his boots properly he gave me a terrible flogging and I went out onto the back steps and pissed in both his army boots with tears steaming down my face. My little sister, Debbie, saw me and ran and told on me, 'Mummy, Mark is widdling in daddy's army boots'. I never was liked by my little 'give up' of a sister. Dad came out and gave me a second hiding.

When I'd done something really bad as a kid my Mum or Dad would say 'Mark, did you do that?' and I'd say, 'No, Errey did it'.

'Who's Errey?' my Mum or Dad would ask, and I'd say 'he's the bloke who comes over to our place and does all the bad stuff'.

'Yes', said my Dad, 'well, when Errey comes back give him this from me' and smash, crash, bash, I'd cop it.

Dr Spock my old man wasn't.

Of course Errey was my little boy imaginary mate and whenever I got caught doing the things all young boys did as part of growing up, such as punching holes in the next door neighbor's car roof with a hammer and a screw driver, or setting fire to the chook shed, or lighting fires in general, setting my little sister's dolls on fire, putting fire crackers down the open petrol tanks of parked cars and pissing in my Dad's boots, it was always 'Errey's' fault.

Errey did it. No-one ever believed me but as a little boy it sounded like a bloody good story to me. Maybe I should have blamed Errey when I was in many and varied police stations not answering questions over a number of different crimes.

'Who set fire to the chook shed?'

'Errey did it.'

'Who's Errey?' Silly question. He's the bloke who comes over here and does all that sort of stuff. No-one ever believed me.

Once when I got caught trying to burn down St Barnabas' Church my Dad nearly killed me after putting out the fire, then when I protested that 'Errey did it' he said: 'Well, how come the matches were in your pocket' and I said: 'Errey gave them to me for me to mind' and Dad laughed and said: 'You're a nut case, son, but at least you stick to your story'. And boy did I stick to it. It got to the point that when I was caught setting fire to the rubbish bins at school and the teachers would scream: 'Who did that?', the other kids would yell: 'Errey did it'.

'Who's Errey?' they would ask. 'He's Chopper's mate', and I'd get six of the best on each hand for my refusal to inform on Errey and give his last name and address. Ha ha.

Then when my Mum and Dad got called in and asked if they knew of my friend 'Errey', my Dad would cover for me claiming that yes, he knew of Errey but didn't know his parents or last name. Then kick me all the way home. Ha ha. Ahhh childhood, what fun it all was.

CHAPTER 33

DEAR CHOPPER...
JAIL MAIL TALES

I HAVE said before that the one big drawback of being in jail is that every bugger knows your address.

I am only allowed to write a certain number of letters per week, yet I receive sometimes over 100 a week, so it stands to reason that a man in jail is unable to answer that much mail.

I get hurt and angry letters from people because I did not answer their other letters. A lot of these people ask me to sign my name so that they can stick it inside their books, or write them a short letter so they can include it with their books.

Please send a photo or letter to me. But understand that I am allowed to write only 15 letters a week and half of them are already spoken for, so it stands to reason that I cannot answer all my mail. Do they think I'm Barbara Cartland with no ears?

People think I am a very rude and thoughtless person for failing to reply. It is impossible to please everyone. I spend half my time in jail with a blooming pen welded to my hand writing, writing, writing. Sometimes I look at a pile of unanswered mail and it all gets too much.

This is mail I fully intended to answer, but I get up and flush the lot down the brasco and say 'consider yourselves posted'. It all gets on top of me at times. Maybe I could get a silent prison. At least I don't have to answer the phones.

It is the same with the visits. I only get half an hour a week now that I am in the mainstream prison, and ten to 20 people a week, who I do not want to come in, arrive at the jail and demand to see old Chop Chop.

This is not a book club, it is a prison. When I say that I don't want to see strangers and use my precious half hour up, they write me a stiff letter of abuse for not seeing them. I can't win.

9.6.94
SOUTH AUSTRALIA, 5158

Dear Mark,

I have just read Chopper Three and I must say that I enjoyed it immensely, so much so that I will purchase your first two books soon.

I was a police officer over here in Adelaide before I left the force in 1990. What I find totally amazing is that your views on drug dealers and child sex offenders don't differ at all from mine, and those of most of the police I used to work with and some of which I still keep in contact with. I, like you, can see the injustice of it all. I can remember a sex offender living in my patrol area. He wasn't fussed whether they were boys or girls providing they were underaged. Anyway, about 10.30 one night while I was on patrol I saw him hanging around the outside of a Kentucky Fried Chicken store as the kids were knocking off.

As soon as he saw the police car he crossed to the other side of the road, so I followed him. He went back to the other side, as did I. I then got out of the car and called to him, and he told me to stop harassing him and that he was going to put in a complaint to I.I.B., which he did.

I was told not to go anywhere near this citizen.

The bleeding hearts and do gooders would have been most pleased with me getting a rap over the knuckles. Another colleague of mine gave the security people at the Westfield Shopping Centre a photocopied picture of this scumbag for them to look out for. The sex offender somehow found out about it, put in a complaint to I.I. Branch. They in turn interviewed the officer involved and were going to charge him with larceny of photocopy paper.

He ended up being charged with a breach of some police general order much to his chagrin. You can see from this Mark that you're not the only one beating your head up against a brick wall.

It must be somewhat off-putting for you getting letters from people all over Australia, knowing that they know all about you and you know nothing about them.

Well I'm 37 years old, separated from my wife, but look after my two little girls, ten and five years of age. My estranged wife is having the girls for four days and it gets lonely without them. So it's time like these that I like to read and catch up on mundane household duties.

I'm an earthmoving operator working for my brother, and a speedway bike referee, so now you know a little about me. I bet you're blown out with excitement.

Well, Chopper, I hope you haven't fallen asleep too many times while reading this. On a final note, I wouldn't worry to much about the idiots who criticise your literary efforts; they would be the same people who would see an Arnold Schwarzenegger film and complain about the acting!

All the best Mark.
Gavin.

MT ELIZA, 3930

23.5.94

Dear Sir,

Firstly let me introduce myself. My name is Andrew, I am 23 years old and have just been discharged from the Army after five years service. I have read all of your books and first heard your name when I too was hanging around the streets of Melbourne, St Kilda in particular.

I am just writing to thank you for teaching me a valuable lesson. Without condemning you or your actions in anyway, or bringing on any unwarranted ridicule, your actions as described in your book have saved me from entering a life of crime.

I was 13 years old in 1984 when my father died, just leaving my mother, my sister and myself. At that early age I had no idea what life or love was all about, but following the death of my father I soon learned. Angry at the world and myself (the night before my father died he found out that I received a Saturday detention at school, subsequently putting some of the blame onto myself). I was looking for someone or something to be part of, a feeling of belonging that I lost when my father died.

It was the same old story that I was very impressionable at that age and I was sucked into the bright lights and mystique of St Kilda and associated with the wrong type of people. I was searching for that male bonding that I felt was cheated from me. Naturally enough fighting became my way of dealing with my aggression and winning somehow justified it. Before too long, my mother was becoming very concerned about my activities, and I acted like the rebel and told her that she didn't know what she was talking about and so forth.

By the time I was 17 years old, I could look after myself fairly well and knew my way around Melbourne and some of the right people. Throughout this whole time I was a private school student and walked a fine line between doing the right thing by my peers and the street kid that was struggling to be contained.

Eventually, it got out and in just three punches I had put a friend of mine in hospital for two weeks.

It was at this time that I began to realise what strength I had, and that I could not always control it. I had seen you before in the Prince of Wales and obviously kept my distance but I also realised that if something didn't change in my life I could see myself being your apprentice. With that in mind I completed school and joined the Army. This was good for me as I felt I could release my aggression and fears by sticking a bayonet into a tyre, and it provided the discipline I needed.

As you say, you are who you are, and the same with me. I still feel a great deal of hurt inside and I began to stray into my former self. I never had a criminal record before the Army and it didn't take me long to notch up my first. Attempted armed robbery, assault with intent to rob, unlawful assault and assault in company. One hell of a way to start out I think. Without going into too much detail all charges were dropped and a new charge was entered to which I pleaded guilty – assault with a weapon.

Believing I was lucky, and had learnt my lesson, that ugly monster reared its head again and I was back in court, this time for threatening unlawful violence and possession of an offensive weapon. I got a 12- month good behaviour bond for both cases and $540 and $300 fines respectively. This time I was lucky.

I even spent 27 days in the Defence Force Corrective Establishment and if jail is worse than that you can have it. D.F.C.E. is a hole. You have to stand to attention to ask permission to have salt and pepper on your meal. What a crock!

I realised that no matter how hard I tried the Army was doing little to discourage my aggression. If anything it encouraged it. I had read your books and had taken quite a liking to them. What I had to do was get away from everything, so I got out of the Army, had a nice holiday for a few months on the Gold Coast, said sorry to Mum for all the shit in the past and came back to Melbourne.

So now I sit here behind my computer studying engineering at university, wearing respectable clothes and driving a nice car, looking forward to the future. I cannot forget the things I have done in the past, as they are tattooed on my body by $6500 worth of ink. I am not proud of what I have done, but I do not regret anything. Life is a learning experience, but experience isn't what you do, it's what you learn from it.

This must sound like chicken feed for you but to me this was pretty major. I mean this with the utmost respect and admiration; in your book you say that your best teacher is your enemy, but in my case it was you. Your mistakes have been my learning points. Think of it this way, your book, by exposing a life in crime, has probably stopped quite a few kids like I was and made them think about where their life was going. Despite all else you must feel some pride in that.

I hope you have not taken offence to anything that I have said, as none was intended and I have said it as a sign of respect. If I have I humbly apologise. I wish you all the best in the future and in particular with your current problem. Please find enclosed a stamp. If you wish to write back to me I would be honored.

If not, I will fully understand and still respect you for it. I am not trying to be patronising, but whether I agree with what you have done is irrelevant. I can only thank you for what you have done for me.

Hey Chopper! If it is any consolation, I believe your are innocent.

Yours sincerely,
Andrew

P.S. I realise that you have no idea who I am, but if you would like anything: newspapers, magazine etc. just write and let me know. I think you are one of the last of the great Australians, for your dedication and loyalty to your mates. This is very rare these days.

MEADOW HEIGHTS, 3048

Dear Mark,

If I may call you that. I am writing you this letter after just finishing your third book. I must give credit where credit is due. All three books were very interesting and well written. I don't know really why I am writing you this letter. I don't know if you'll read it. I hope you will find the time.

You're probably thinking you have all the time in the world. Well I don't. In my opinion, not that it counts much, I feel you should be set free. I, like a lot of other people, feel you are not a threat to anyone. Well you do know what I mean. I can't understand why they still have you behind those walls. I hope everything works out for you as I feel you have done the people of Victoria a great deal.

Well, I will tell you a bit about myself. I am a 22-year-old female. I have two children, a girl aged four named Sharlene and a son aged 22 months named Daniel. I no longer see the father of my children. I am Maltese. By the way in one of your books you said the typical Maltese girl always goes for the kitchen knife. After reading that I stopped and thought for a while; it is so true, as I always reach for the stay sharp. It would have to be my best friend in the kitchen. I haven't had to use it yet. Anyway my hobbies would have to be cars, reading and my kids. As you have noticed I have sent no photos. I am not going to make any promises that I know I can't keep.

All I ask from you is to read my letters. I'm not even going to ask you to be my friend as I'm sure you've had enough 'friends'. I will ask you to please try to write to me. I can understand you probably get so much mail and you would get sick of writing. If you can find the time I would be grateful.

Before I finish this letter I would like to thank you for making me and many others realise what kind of place we really live in.

You are one of a kind Chopper but I am glad you wrote those books and I am sorry the Australian Governments are so stupid. I hope to hear from you soon. I am sure I can arrange that cardigan too.

Send me a size if you send me a line.

Yours,
Elaine

26.4.94

PETRIE, 4502

Chopper,

Hi there! How's life? First of all I have to say that your third book was brilliant. It's about the only book I've read twice cover to cover. You've gotta do a fourth book. I haven't read the first two, but I'm getting them from the library and then I'll probably buy them.

Yeah, I guess I'll buy 'em. I'm sure they'll be just as good as the third.

I almost got the third book confiscated for reading it in a science lesson. But fortunately student teachers are real dickheads and believe everything you tell them. This one was no exception. Guess which was more interesting. I mean, who gives a shit about physics and crap like that. I mean it's not gonna help me when I get out of school.

When will anybody ask you 'What's the average velocity … Blah blah blah.'

Do you know where you can get 'Chopper T-Shirts'. Not many shops know what you're talking about when you ask. They all sort of stare at you and then say stuff like 'Oh the only HD shirts we have are on the shelves.' I mean I don't want a bloody Harley shirt, I want a Chopper shirt.

What do you expect from a private schoolgirl? I'm sure you'll have heaps of jokes. Want to tell me some? I'm sure the school needs a few more cultural, tasteful jokes. You know, the ones you hear in jail. When's your birthday? I'm not offended easily so tell me the worst jokes you know. I know this sounds weird but I reckon you look stranger with ears than you do without (no offence or anything). I'm sure people have said worse. I've gotta go.

Katrina

PS. If someone was really crook and wanted to meet you would they be able to say through the 'make a wish foundation', or through the 'starlight foundation' that they'd like to meet Chopper. Would you be allowed to come up?

7.5.94

Chopper,

Yep it's your little posh private school girl here. I should be able to read your two books in about a month because the library had to have them rebound because they were worn out too much.

At the moment I'm in hospital so I can't send a photo in this letter. Probably in the next one. I don't know about you but I hate photos and so I smile crappily for photos. Photos are not my thing. But I'll send it next letter O.K. Thanks for the photos. I'll definitely treasure them for ever. Believe me, I'm not laughing at the shorts or what's in the shorts. There's more to you than meets the eye. Somehow I can't see you looking after those roses though, I can see you saying 'Oh, these roses ain't got enough flowers, out you go' or something like that. No, leave the looking after the flowers to the bum chums.

At this moment we're having a wet tissue fight in the room. Shit, what a laugh. There are these two guys and me in the room throwing these things at each other. I wish I was a better shot. I missed the Goddamn pricks and they got me all the time. It's not fair. Bugger 'em. Who were your friends in the photos - say hello! Does anyone look at the letters before you? Hello to those arseholes!

Hello from Alana

That's Alana, she's seven and is in hospital too. She's a sweetie. I've got some more jokes! Equally as polite as the last set (of course).

What's Michael Jackson have in common with a bottle of whisky? They both come in little tots.

Hi Mark (Chopper) Read, I have heard a lot about you on *A Current Affair,* about what you have done. I am glad what you are trying to do for our country and the children's future. Good luck in the future. From **Shane,** your new pal.

That's Shane, he's 16.

Hi, I have heard a lot about you Mr Chopper, I liked your joke, I have some jokes, anyway got to go – **Mitchell.**

Hi, Mr Chopper, how are you? Hope ya good. As you've probably guessed I'm in hospital too! I'm 13. What do you do all day? If it is like here, ya' just sit on ya' arse all day doing nothing. It sux. I hope ya' fine. – **Anna.**

So there you go. You've got a fan club in hospital. You should have seen Brad's (a nurse) face when he saw the photos of you. He went ghost white when he saw ya'. Shane goes to him, 'Seen him before?' and Brad goes 'Who hasn't?'

Take it as an compliment. Do tattoos hurt? Everyone likes the joke even Brad laughed. We (Shane, Mitch and me) had a coughing fit all through the joke. We were in hysterics whenever we thought of the head just sitting on the pillow and the nurse saying 'You'll have to speak up, he's deaf'. I just about pissed myself. Know any others? Do tell. Would it offend you if I showed my friends your letters? What's the food like in there? If it's anything like hospital food I feel sorry for ya! Hospital food tastes like shit. I don't know anyone who likes it.

In hospital there's not much to do but sit on your arse or watch TV. We go to school for a few hours everyday, but it's basically a bludge. Same there? Apart from the fact that when I get better I can leave and you can't (yet) hospital is a jail. I am stuck here at their mercy to let me go. Here's Anna.

Hi Chopper! How are you again. Katrina just told me this is the same letter and guess when and where she's writing it? 11.40am at school. Shane's giving us a geography lesson and is acting like a real dickhead. School sux as usual, school teacher's coming. I gotta go. Good luck. **Anna.**

The work is so boring so I'm just saying I don't have any books so I can't do it.

Hi again, we have to wait for the teacher and I'm getting bored. Do you know that Katrina has cystic fibrosis. I'll let her tell you about it herself. I have five diseases. Chronic fatigue syndrome (CFS), fibro myalga, irritable bowel syndrome, heartburn, asthma. CFS makes you tired all the time and you sleep your life away. It makes your muscles tired so sometimes it's hard to move. Fibro myalga makes your brain send the wrong messages to your muscles which twist them, it really hurts. When I get them in my head I scream. It gives me migraines that make you spew and affects your colon (large intestine) so you get really bad stomach aches. Other symptoms are dizziness, headaches, loss of being able to concentrate, wreck your eye muscles and all the other muscles, so I may get my own wheel chair. I could die, but I won't (I hope).

Irritable bowel syndrome – things go straight through me.

Reflux – makes me spew.

School finishes in five mins! Sleeptime. I might write again later. Take care.

Anna

Dear Mark,

Sorry I have no 'bum view' g-string poses for you or even a tattoo of your book's cover on my back, but being a 15-year-old schoolgirl makes it a little illegal (and besides I don't really want to).

You've (by the sound of it) heard 'Chopper you've got a great little book here' a million times but I'm going to say it again. Your book's content and style of writing are both great. I think you have a wonderful way with words.

Did you do well in English at school?.

You make violence humorous (which scares me a little). Did you have much trouble getting a lot of your books content published?

I've no idea what gave me the courage to write this letter. I guess telling friends and family how great a book is just doesn't have the same effect as telling the author the same thing.

I am fascinated by your life, as you have lived such a vivacious and fulfilling life (so it seems) and I'd like to do the same with my life (without all the weapons, violence, whores, pimps, AIDS and Italians wearing slip-on shoes) ... all the friends you've made make it sound so ace (except for Sid).

I wish you well and hope that you find the time to write back to me.

PS. You have no idea how many Telecom bitches it took to get your address.

PSS. I think you were a cute baby with cute ears.

Donna

17.4.94

Dear Mark,

Do you get many letters from people you don't know. Or do you get letters from people you WISH you didn't know? I hope this one doesn't fall into either of those categories!

I hear you're a bit of a writer Mark, that's a real gift. I'm afraid my writing talent is non-existent, but I felt urged to write you a few lines.

You and I are pretty much the same you know. Does that sound unbelievable especially as I know next to nothing about you? Yet I can say it confidently! However, there is one difference. Ah, here it comes, I hear you say. Is it because I'm out here and you are in there? Or … I'm sure you can think of a dozen or two differences between us but I can only see one that really matters for all time – my sins are forgiven. So what!

Let me tell you a story before you throw this across the room. There were two beggars. One wandered off and a while later came back to his mate saying 'I've found bread! I want to share it with you so come on and I'll show you how to find it!'.

'No way' says his mate, 'you just think you're better than me because you've got bread now'.

'You're wrong,' says the beggar. 'I'm not any better than you – but I am better off than you because I have found what I've been looking for.'

So Mark, I'm not better than you in God's sight – all sin is black, no matter what, but through Jesus I've found forgiveness, peace and a new life. Won't you follow me to the bread of life and like me, you'll never be hungry again. You're captive but so was I. Now I'm free and you can be too! Jesus says 'Then you will know the truth, and the truth will set you free'. (John 8 verse 32) and 'I am the way, the truth and the life. No-one comes to the Father except through me'. (John 14 verse 6).

If I am wrong, Mark, what have I lost. I'll have lived a fulfilled life. But if you are wrong you'll have lost your eternal life. I know I'm not wrong Mark, trust me and him who sent me.

Thank you for allowing me into your life Mark to share my joy with you.

Maureen

CHAPTER 34

THE FIGHT TO WRITE

THE General Manager of Corrective Services, Mr Ben Marris, sent me a letter telling me not to write a book. So much for free speech. This is what it said:

Dear Mr Read, *'I refer to your letters of 7.1.94 and 19.1.94, in which you request permission to write a book. It is in the policy of this department that a prisoner should not, while under sentence, profit in any way from his crime. I am advised that your previous books have been concerned with crime and it would seen probable that any future book that you wrote would attempt to capitalise upon such notoriety as you have achieved through crime. For this reason permission to write a book is refused.'* – Yours sincerely, Ben Marris.

The letter was headed Department of Justice, Corrective Services Division. Well, I guess that calls a halt to my literary career. Oh well, I will put the matter to my lawyers, but to be quite honest I'm getting a bit sick of banging my head up against a brick wall.

I've got too much on my mind to cope with this shit at the moment.

What really got up my nose is when he said he was advised that my previous books had been about crime. It would have been nice if he had popped down the road and bought a couple. I could do with the royalties. I have a hungry family of lawyers to feed.

This book has been put together under great difficulty, letter by letter, page by page, under the nose of prison security.

They have banned me from writing a book. No doubt I will be punished when this comes out. I think the chances of getting the prison governor to launch this particular volume are very skinny. The authorities have told me they have banned me from writing because they think it is not right for me to 'profit from crime'. Here am I, trying to clear my name, using some of the country's highest paid lawyers and the state is banning me from paying my way.

If I had sat on my arse, watching the soapies on the TV and doing nothing, I could have got legal aid and the taxpayers would have had to pay my legal bills.

But I have paid every cent, myself, from my book royalties. I am now broke, and the government wants to stop me doing the only thing I can to make an honest dollar. They condemn me when I shorten the shoe size of drug-dealing vermin, yet they stop me from writing.

I work in the prison laundry for a few bucks a month. A lawyer would tip a waiter more than I get paid in jail each week, yet the authorities stop me from trying to earn enough to pay lawyers instead of being a drain on the public purse.

I am told I could fight the decision to stop me writing by going to the international court in the United Nations. But what would be the point. No-one wants to fight for the rights of a former headhunter who wants to write for a living. The truth is that people like to read what I write. Modesty forbids me from saying that my first three books have all been bestsellers. Why should a few prison guards and Government shinybums stop me from doing what I do second best?

They have always told me that the pen is mightier than the sword, and at last I'm getting the idea. So instead of fighting them in the courts I have had to use other, sneakier, less costly methods.

Letters have been sent to various addresses and then forwarded on to my publishers. Every letter I write and send out has been held up by prison security, and read and re-read to decide if that particular letter could be used for a book. It was my writing letters in relation to Henry Lawson and Banjo Paterson that finally convinced prison staff that my mail was just harmless stuff not meant for any book. And I know that because one particular security officer – who is in no danger of becoming a brain surgeon – said to me, 'I am getting a bit sick of reading your bloody mail, Chopper. If it's not about Henry Lawson you are on about Banjo Paterson, but at least we can see that you are not trying to write a book.' Everyone's a critic, hey? Ha ha.

I must confess that some of my letters and a lot of photos have gone out of the jail in a covert manner. Once the fourth book is published I doubt I will ever be able to get away with a fifth while I am still in jail. So, dear reader, if this fourth effort appears somewhat insanely put together, please forgive me and remember that it has been written by the only writer in Australia today who has been prohibited from writing books, by the light of a television set late at night.

In saying goodbye may I quote the immortal words of Bob Dylan:

Mama put my guns in the ground, I can't shoot them any more,
That long black cloud keeps coming down ,
I feel I'm knocking on heaven's door.

MY LAST POEM

So my writing upsets the toffs, the politicians and the cops,
But when ya jump on the horse, ya flog her till she drops,
And I guess now I will have to call it quits,
It's hard yakka brother, and I must say it's giving me the shits,
I've written about mugs and molls and ladies of easy persuasion,
About the poets of old, and the cultural yank invasion,
I've written about the pros and cons of every bloomin' thing,
Knocked up songs no man will ever sing,
And every word's been done with just a touch of comic malice,
And all from my little cell in the old Pink Palace.
But the time has come to turn it up, 'cos it's messing up my mind,
And as my old Dad used to say, 'Stop it son, or you'll go blind',
So this is it, I swear to God, and of that I am quite certain,
I've written down my last verse, reached my final curtain,
It's time to toss my pen and paper in the fire.
But you and me both know that I'm a shocking liar,
And it's easy to see if you look at me,
And all the times I've been busted,
That when I say I'll walk away ...
You know I can't be trusted.
Ha ha.